# The Magic of
# Getting What You Want

# The Magic of GETTING WHAT YOU WANT

# David J. Schwartz

WILSHIRE BOOK COMPANY
9731 VARIEL AVENUE
CHATSWORTH, CALIFORNIA 91311

Published by arrangement with HarperCollins Publishers.
All rights reserved.

Copyright © 1983 by David Schwartz

Library of Congress Cataloging in Publication Data

Schwartz, David Joseph.
The magic of getting what you want.

Includes index.
1. Success.   2. Conduct of life.     I. Title.
HF5386.S412     1983     650.1     82-23989
ISBN 0-688-01824-6

Printed in the United States of America

2   3   4   5   6   7   8   9   10

BOOK DESIGN BY ELLEN LO GIUDICE

## FOR DAVID JAMES

When he was about eighteen months old, David James spent an afternoon with me. Young David loved to test his strength. So we played the game of arm-wrestle. David, of course, won at least three matches in four.

Finally, after "losing" so often, I said to David, "Okay, we'll do this only one more time."

And then David said to me very affirmatively, "No, PaPa. *Two* more ones!!"

"No, PaPa. *Two* more ones." A tremendous concept! Don't you agree?

To David James then, to his wonderful sisters, Sara Ann and Abigail Amanda, to their parents, David Jefferson and Ann Shanks, and to each of you who wants "*two* more ones," two times as much love, happiness, respect, appreciation, and money, I dedicate this book.

The philosophy works!

David Joseph Schwartz

# Contents

# Think More About Having More

Think about it. Every challenge we face can be solved by a dream. Let me explain.

Consider for a moment what you want. Chances are you want more money so you can enjoy more of the good things this life can offer—a nicer home, more respect on and off the job, more love, more vacations more plain old-fashioned happiness.

You want to do more for your mate, share more good times, build more financial security, enjoy more time together. You want more years to live, better health.

You want to give more to your children—more good education, more cultural advantages, more opportunities to excel and be the best they can be.

The dream of thinking more is the key to your personal prosperity and enthusiasm for life. It is also the answer to making mankind better and healthier, and to building an economy of plenty. Farmers who want to earn more money figure out ways to get more bushels of grain per acre, more eggs per chicken, more milk per cow. Successful manufacturers continually search for ways to produce more per employee, more per hour, and more with less raw material.

Thinking more is even the best answer to crime. As some people state so well, it is not the love of money but the lack of money that is the root of evil. People who learn how easy and self-fulfilling it is to earn more in any one of a thousand ways are not candidates for the courts and penitentiaries.

Thinking more is responsible for the degree of civilization we have attained. Thinking of a better life got us out of the caves. It brought us electricity, telephones, automobiles, and airplanes. Those who think more have reason to be concerned about those who think less—the people who say, "Be satisfied with who you are and what you have and learn to tolerate misery, unhappiness, failure." For such people, life may as well be a prison sentence that will never end until death.

## Decide to Go for Utopia

Utopia means the perfect place where there is love, health, peace, wealth, and happiness—a land beyond description. Most people believe we cannot find or create utopia on earth. In fact, the word *utopia,* coined by Sir Thomas More, comes from two Greek words which, combined, mean "no place."

Utopia is beyond the reach of our society until we overcome the obstacles that stand in our way. And what are these obstacles? Negativism, fear, depression, and the problems they create—discouragement, economic stagnation, crime, drug dependency, family distrust, and many more.

Some argue that we are moving away from utopia at a rapid rate. Each decade we set new records for drug and alcohol abuse, divorce, murder, rape, suicide, and a host of other problems, which suggests that society is getting worse, not better.

Now utopia may be beyond the reach of an entire society. But you are not an entire society. You, as an individual or as a family, can come very close indeed to achieving your utopia.

Let me describe a couple of people determined to create their own utopia who are making real progress.

## How an Immigrant Is Building a Cab Company

Recently, I was in an Atlanta suburb during rush hour and needed a cab. Finally, one stopped and I got in. The cab was very clean but very old—a twenty-year-old Cadillac. The driver said, "Good evening, sir, where may I take you?" I told him where I wanted to go and then I said, "You're from Jamaica, aren't you?"

He glanced quickly at me and said, "Why, yes, I am, but how did you know?"

"I get to Jamaica frequently," I explained, "and your accent is unmistakably Jamaican. I love it."

We drove through the traffic for a few minutes without speaking, and then the driver said very affirmatively, "This my cab. I own it. I am in business for myself. Soon I will own two cabs. My dream is to own twenty cabs."

I said, "Great. I'm always glad to meet an entrepreneur. How long have you lived in the United States?"

"Eleven months," he replied. "When I got to this country, I had two hundred dollars, and already I have my own business."

My mind immediately reflected on a newspaper headline I'd seen while waiting for the cab. It said "9,200,000 People Are Unemployed." I thought to myself: How could this fellow who is in a strange, new environment have a successful business when a staggering number of people who were born and educated here are unemployed?

"You're a remarkable fellow," I said. "You must work very hard."

"Oh, no, sir," he replied. "This isn't work. I like what I'm doing. You see, the profits all come to me, not to a boss or some big company. As you said, I am an entrepreneur, and someday I will enjoy a very good life."

After he dropped me off, I thought: Here is a fellow who appreciates what the system has to offer and is giving it his best. He may not reach his own utopia, but he is going to come awfully close.

## Going into Business for Herself Put "That Utopian Spirit" into Jan

Fortunately, there is a wave of new converts to utopianism among your neighbors and mine. These people are discovering that a much better, happier, and more financially rewarding life is within reach. Let me tell you about Jan.

For many years, I have presented a seminar on "Self-direction for Personal Growth," here and in foreign countries. The people who attend come from the big corporations, small businesses, government agencies—all walks of life. One day, in the O'Hare Airport in Chicago, I met a woman who had attended my seminar in Washington, D.C.

As I walked through a corridor, I heard someone call my name. I looked around, saw no one I knew, and kept on walking. Then I heard someone calling my name again. I stopped, looked again. I saw an attractive woman running down the corridor smiling and waving at me.

In a few seconds, she grabbed my arm and said, "Dr. Schwartz, how are you?" I replied, "I'm great, how are you?" She said, "I'm fantastic. It's so good to see you again." Then, as we continued walking, I said, "I'm sorry, but I don't remember meeting you." (I've learned it's usually best to admit not knowing someone who knows you.)

"Well," she answered, "we've never met face-to-face, but I took your self-direction seminar in Washington four years ago. It changed my life! My name is Jan F. Do you have time for coffee?"

I said, "Sure. I've got an hour before my flight to San Francisco."

"Good," she said. "I've got ninety minutes until my flight departs."

Jan soon told me that she was in business for herself. I asked her to tell me about it.

"Well, I had acquired a lot of background about the Social Security system in my ten years in the agency. I saw a need to provide a service to businesses advising them on how they could reduce Social Security costs. In my years with Social Security, I learned that some businesses were paying more Social Security taxes than are legally required.

"For the next six months following your seminar," Jan went on, "after work, I devoted every evening and weekend to deciding what specific money-saving services I could offer and how I could best market them.

"I decided to market my services initially to trade associations, because they represent many businesses and are eager to present money-saving ideas to their members," Jan continued.

"I quit working for Social Security just three years ago yesterday."

"I'm eager to know how you're doing," I asked. "You certainly look happy and prosperous."

"I am happy and I am prospering," she emphasized. "I'm happy because I love what I'm doing. I often work seventy hours a week, but work isn't 'work' anymore. It's fun. I'm traveling all over meeting other people who also enjoy what they do.

"And I'm well into six figures a year already, although I've barely made a dent in the potential market for my services. I've got four people working with me now, and I give each of them a piece of the action because I want them to put forth their very best efforts, too. And it's working. When compensation is based on performance, people just plain do better."

"But wasn't it hard to break away from Social Security?" I asked.

"I confess it took courage to break away," Jan replied. "I was giving up security, and the pay wasn't all that bad. On top of that, I was saying good-bye to a routine I understood. I knew my job. But as I evaluated my situation, I asked myself some sobering questions. I still keep them in my briefcase."

Jan handed me her questions. Here they are:

1. What was the fixed routine doing to my ambition? Would I be happy at the end of my career knowing that I had never really tested myself to see what I could create?

2. What were the people I associated with day in and day out doing to my overall attitudes? What damage was being done to my mind by hearing the same complaints about how unfair the system is, why so-and-so should not have been promoted, and the petty talk at coffee breaks and lunch?

3. To whom did I owe the bigger obligation—to myself or to the organization?

4. Was I really enjoying my free time? Could my free time be better spent?

I told Jan I'd like to have a copy of her questions for use in my work. She agreed, and immediately went to a copy machine and returned with a copy for me.

Soon the hour was almost up and I had to hurry to catch my plane. The conversation with Jan had reinforced my view that thinking more is magnificent and the trip to utopia is exciting.

## How to Profit by Writing Your Obituary

An obituary is supposed to be a brief history of a person's life. Usually, it gives only the barest details, such as date and place of birth, main accomplishments, occupation, and next of kin.

For obvious reasons, most people do not like to write their obituaries. Nevertheless, I've turned obituary writing into a success-building concept for use in seminars for managers.

Here's how it works. I ask the managers to write a summary of where they have been to date in their lives—with added information about family, friends, work, and finances. Then I ask them to write projected versions of the rest of their lives based on past performances. I've learned that our past behavior is a good indicator of where we are headed unless we take positive corrective actions.

The obituary idea works. Let me give you one example. Just after taking off on a flight from Chicago to New York recently, a man in the aisle seat across from me said, "Pardon me, are you Dr. Schwartz?" I smiled and replied, "I was when I got up this morning."

The fellow introduced himself and said, "Well, I remember you from a seminar you conducted six years ago. In particular, I remember that overnight assignment, the "'write your own obituary'" exercise. At the time, I thought the idea was stupid, but I went along with it. It changed my life."

"Tell me how," I said.

"Well," my friend began, "looking back on my life and what I had done with it made me mad at myself. I was thirty-nine at the time, and in writing my obituary, I had to admit to myself certain negatives in my life. I realized I wasn't giving my wife and two kids as much attention as they deserved and needed. Most of my friends were depressing—the 'everything is bad and getting rapidly worse' types."

"What about work and finances?" I asked.

"My analysis of my accomplishments in my work were really negative," my friend continued. "I'm an engineer, and if I had applied myself, I would have been a partner in the firm. But I didn't. And in the money department, I had accumulated little more than some equity in our home."

"Once you had analyzed your life history to that point, what did you do?" I asked.

"You'll recall that the obituary exercise you assigned asked us to project the future based on the past unless we took positive corrective action. The only conclusion I could reach was that my life and the lives of people close to me would only become increasingly miserable down the road. So, immediately on returning home from the seminar, I decided to take some of that positive corrective action, and it worked. I paid more attention to my family and our relationship now is great. I developed new friends—positive types. I began to apply myself at work and now I am a partner, and as for my finances, I'm doing very, very well."

After we parted in the airport, I thought to myself: None of us can change the past. But we can change the future when we take positive corrective action.

Success does begin with a dream of more.

## Poverty Is Poor People Who Lack a Dynamic Dream

It is no disgrace to be poor, but not having money, resenting the fact that some other people do, and having no concrete dream for improving one's circumstances is totally deflating.

To state it differently, there are two kinds of poor people: individuals with little money and no hope for acquiring it, and individuals with little financial wherewithal but who have a dream for making it.

Many parents discourage their children from trying to find the really good life on the grounds that it's impossible, so they should be content to settle for an ordinary job and the average existence it provides. These parents don't tell their children that every rich family was, in this generation or in a past generation, poor. Huge, prosperous businesses such as McDonald's, Ford, Kentucky Fried Chicken, and Amway were started by people with very little capital. Furthermore, Presidents Coolidge, Hoover, Truman, Eisenhower, Johnson, Nixon, Ford, Carter, and Reagan—all except two of the people who led the nation in modern times—were born to poor or modestly well-off parents. Presidents Roosevelt and Kennedy were the only exceptions.

## Thought Leaders Tell Us to Think Less— Not More

The people who shape the thinking for most of us claim that times are bad and getting worse, society is about to collapse, war is a certainty, crime will only increase, and new exotic diseases will get us sooner or later.

Many thought leaders—teachers, economists, editorial writers, novelists, critics, politicians, and planners—specialize in spreading the bad news. Teachers tell students to seek jobs that offer security and good fringe benefits—not jobs that spell opportunity and reward based on performance. Many economists forecast economic collapse and urge us to fill our basements or rent a miniwarehouse and stock it with nonperishable food; editorial writers and critics find fault with most proposals that would make life better; and politicians specialize in promising us something for nothing.

None of us can control society or the economy. But each of us can determine our own destiny, our own economic condition, and our own happiness. How to achieve control over what happens to us is the central message of this book. Follow the guidelines and watch good things happen!

## Decide to Scale Up, Not Scale Down

For the better part of a generation, proponents of negative thought have been telling us to cut back—to be satisfied with miniature housing units, cars built for dwarfs, near-frigid in-home temperatures in the winter and sweat-producing temperatures in the summer. In brief, they've been saying we're running out of energy, living space, resources, and money. They tell us to "learn to enjoy a lower standard of living, because the good life is behind us."

These prophets of gloom even make it sound patriotic to do with less. Carried to the extreme, these do-with-less folks would soon have us living five to a room and would allot us the Russian housing standard of one hundred square feet per person.

Recently, I read one of those back-to-the-cave essays in *Time*. Part of the conclusion to the article stated, "The current construction of their housing may make some Americans claustrophobic, but cross-cultural comparison might also remind them to be grateful for what they have."[1] In other words, despite how unhappy you may be with your dwelling unit, be happy because it's better than a house in some economically underdeveloped nation.

Such a view is nonsense. It is of little comfort to a sick person to learn that he or she is not as sick as someone else. Worse, it helps lower our standard of living, because it reduces the size of our thinking.

Fortunately, there are still some of us who are determined to use all the skill and all the belief we have in the better life and fight the live-in-a-hut mentality. Interestingly, facing the "downsize the American dream" essay in *Time* was a full-color ad by Oldsmobile. The ad pictured a full-sized Oldsmobile and began with this statement: "Families deserve the nicer things in life, too."

The advertisement went on to describe how luxurious, roomy, and comfortable the car is.

Besides showing a beautiful automobile, the ad also pictured a fine home, not a mansion but a very nice house, one that could be owned by anyone who makes a commitment to thinking more, not less.

To me, the contrast between the do-with-less-and-like-it essay and the beautiful ad stressing the good life gives us a choice. Do we want to settle in, accept the monotonous, go-nowhere life? Or do we choose to think more and enjoy our life to the maximum?

---

[1]Lance Morrow, "Downsizing the American Dream," *Time*, October 5, 1981, p. 96.

## Think More—Not Less—to Solve Budget Problems

Today, all over the world, individuals, couples, companies, and governments are trying to solve budget problems. The basic problem is always the same. People spend more than they take in as income.

Nearly always the solution people find to a budget problem is the same—and wrong. Consider this conversation between Jane and Bill.

Jane: "We're falling way behind in our monthly payments. We've simply got to cut down on our spending."

Bill: "You're right. But where?"

Jane: "Well, we can stop going out on weekends. And we can cancel the vacation we've planned. Maybe we can find a way to reduce the fuel bills. And you call your mother a lot long distance."

On and on it goes. Balance the budget by thinking less, cutting back, denying yourself what you want.

There is no harm in "Waste not, want not," but thinking in terms of less is not the solution. Recently, I was in a savings and loan bank. The bank was giving away a packet of twelve brochures on how to improve your fiscal fitness. I took them home and examined them. Each brochure told the reader how to save money by doing with less—less food, less heat, fewer auto expenses, cheaper education for the kids.

Not one of those pamphlets suggested one idea about how to make more money to solve a budget problem and create financial independence!

Some corporate managers follow the same procedure as Bill and Jane.

President: "Projected revenue for next year is off by twenty percent. Now how can we cut our costs so we can balance our budget?"

Mr. Squeakie: "Sir, we can cut out our training program. It won't pay off for at least two years."

Mr. Miser: "And let's cut way back on research and development. Nobody knows for sure if that new product we're designing will make money."

Mr. Tightwad: "We should give up paying the bonuses this year. After all, we pay enough in salaries. Why spoil our people with extra compensation?"

Now a progressive company dedicated to the concept of more will figure out ways to increase revenue so the budget is not only balanced, but a profit results.

Concentrate on earning more, not on stretching your income to the point that you are denied what you want.

One fellow explained his budget problem to me this way. He said, "I was spending at least ten hours a week trying to figure out ways to cut back, skimp, and somehow get by on my income. And I was losing two hours or more every night lying in bed worrying about how badly off I was and what would happen to my family and me.

"Then I got my head turned around. I got a part-time job and now it is paying almost as much as my regular job. I have almost doubled my income in six months and I'm a whole lot happier and I'm enjoying life far more."

## Seek Out Dream Builders—Avoid the Dream Destroyers

For decades, I have had the privilege of meeting and observing at close range thousands of people from amazingly different backgrounds. Some were well educated in the academic sense; some had almost no formal education. Some came from wealthy families, while others were products of poverty. The people I have met represented hundreds of occupations, many nationalities, and a variety of personal philosophies.

A minority of the people I met were highly successful

in earning money, rearing families, and winning respect. The majority were not.

Why? After a lot of study, I reached these conclusions. The minority who make it, the doers, the winners, develop big dreams and seek out people who encourage them in pursuit of their goals. Meanwhile, the majority who are wasting their lives either have no meaningful dreams or, if they do, they surround themselves with dream destroyers, people who laugh at them for thinking big, people who have "proof" the dream is unattainable.

Let's examine the most common dream destroyers and consider how you can cope with them if you want to reap the rewards of thinking more.

*Dream Destroyer #1: You don't have enough education.* Education up to a point is useful and necessary for many occupations. But to believe that more formal education is a guarantee of advancement, money, and peace of mind is foolish. Some of the people who head America's five hundred largest corporations never went to college. Meanwhile, many who received advanced degrees are employed as modestly paid corporate hired hands. Education correlates poorly with success. I made a study of twenty-one of my former students who are now worth at least a million dollars—all self-made. Sixteen of them finished college with a C average (the same average President Eisenhower earned at West Point) and five earned a B average; not one graduated with an A average.

A lot of talented people are held back by folks who keep preaching, "Get more formal education." It is significant, I think, that many successful journalists and writers did not study writing in a formal sense. Nor did all successful artists study painting, nor did all successful actors study acting in college.

Think twice before you accept the advice, "Go back to school and study some more."

*Dream Destroyer #2: You don't have enough capital to start your own business.* Not since the early part of the twentieth century have so many people dreamed of owning their own businesses. And never before have so many would-be entrepreneurs had their dreams shattered by people who told them, "You haven't got enough money. Forget your idea."

Not having enough capital is an excuse created by people who themselves lack the power to dream, to use their imagination creatively. A young woman came to me three years ago to ask for help. Her dream was to make and market a line of fine blouses. She explained to me that after talking to an accountant and a representative of the Small Business Administration, she had learned the minimum initial capital required would be between $150,000 and $200,000.

"Dr. Schwartz," she said, "there is no way I can come up with that much money."

"How much capital do you have?" I asked.

"About five thousand dollars," she replied.

"Okay," I said, "if your dream is firmly in place, you can start a blouse business with five thousand dollars." I then explained how she could contract with a garment manufacturer to make a sample line for little capital and how she could market the blouse samples through agents who would work on a straight commission.

To make a fascinating story short, in just three years she has turned her dream into a five-million-dollar-a-year business. And her dream is expanding. Her goal for three years from now is to run a fifty-million-dollar-a-year enterprise.

Even more spectacular is the experience of a good friend of mine. A decade ago, he was deep in debt and even deeper in despair. Then someone persuaded him to get in the Amway business because he could make an extra sixty dollars per month that would help supplement his schoolteacher's salary. With less than a hundred-dollar investment, he got into the business. Did he succeed? Well, last summer he moved into a magnificent, custom-designed, twenty-room house. He enjoys trips all over the world and is watching his success grow!

Next time someone tells you, "You don't have enough capital," get advice from a dream builder, not a dream destroyer.

*Dream Destroyer #3: You're a dreamer. You've got to be realistic in this world.* Chances are you've heard this dream buster many times. But analyze it. Everything begins with a dream. Every business, every building, highway, school, church, house—everything, absolutely everything, is a dream before it becomes a reality. Supercautious people never achieve because they are afraid to dream about what they want to accomplish.

Suppose Wernher von Braun had listened to the people who laughed at his ambitions to put men on the moon? Or suppose Henry Ford had followed the counsel of his closest associates and not tried to build a car everyone could afford?

Dreams come in all sizes and types. Many people are unable to dream of overcoming a serious ailment. And they don't. Others with the same problem dream they can and health returns. Some people in very ordinary jobs can't visualize themselves as moving into management. And they don't. Other ordinary workers see themselves as some day occupying key jobs and they do.

You see, when life is boiled down to its essentials, we find that dreams are the raw material of reality.

Next time someone tells you that you are foolish to dream, analyze that person, and you'll probably find that he or she is mediocre, achieving next to nothing, unadmired, and not the kind of person you would like to be.

Now we all need advice. But accept it only from people who believe in the miraculous power of dreams.

*Dream Destroyer #4: The field is overcrowded. There's too much competition.* Suppose you decide to go into business or enter a profession. Odds are many people around you will say to you, "Look, the field is overcrowded and the failure rate is very high. Don't do it."

The restaurant business is often described as being overcrowded, with one of the highest failure rates of any kind of business. But a young friend of mine, after escaping from Russia, didn't know this. He dreamed of making a fortune in the United States. But how? Well, Isaac knew something about the restaurant business. So, with his meager savings, he opened up a sandwich shop. Between eleven A.M. and three P.M. he does a great business. Now he is in the process of opening three more sandwich shops. His dream is to sell more sandwiches and companion items than anyone else in the city. His goal of making a million dollars within two years is assured. And he's only been in the United States three years!

Another young man I met about five years ago came to me with a problem. He said, "Dr. Schwartz, I want to be a lawyer, but my family, my friends, and the counseling service all tell me I'd be a fool to become a lawyer. The field is absolutely overcrowded. We have more lawyers per thousand people than any other nation."

I agreed with him that we do have a surplus of people who are authorized to practice law. Then I asked him, "Do you really want to practice law?" He replied, "More than anything else. I want to be a top-notch lawyer. But I can only afford to go to a night law school, since I've got three kids to support."

I assured him that graduates of "name" law schools get the jobs in the prestigious law firms, but they don't necessarily make the best lawyers. My friend was surprised to learn that most of the members of the United States Supreme Court graduated from very ordinary, virtually unknown law schools.

My friend put action behind his dream. And he's now moving rapidly to make that dream come true.

*Dream Destroyer #5: You haven't got the time.* There are many opportunities for people to develop sideline ventures in their spare time—ventures that can make money, produce a lot of fun, and do not in any way interfere with a person's regular employment. But again, when you discuss your dream of making several thousand dollars a year more, your dream-destroying friends will tell you, among other negatives, that you don't have time.

Let me tell you about Jim and Alice and how they found time to create a highly profitable part-time business. Jim worked in a bank and Alice operated a word processor in an insurance company. They had a chance to set up their own business. Jim and Alice came to see me to learn how they might find more time. Here were the five suggestions I made:

1. Limit your television viewing to thirty minutes a day. They had been averaging three and a half hours, so this freed up eighteen hours in a six-day week.

2. Stop the daily newspaper. You won't miss it after a week. Another thirty minutes per day saved, or three hours per week.

3. Cut back on your sleep time by thirty minutes per night. Most people, especially when bored, oversleep.

4. Arrange with your managers at work to let you cut your lunch period from sixty minutes to thirty minutes so you can go home thirty minutes early. Over five days, this meant two and a half hours.

5. Cut out those "friends" who insist on calling you

several times a week to complain about how awful the economy is, how badly they are treated at work, and how terrible they feel. This produced savings of one and a half hours per week.

The net result was that Jim and Alice each found twenty-eight and a half extra hours per week. Plenty of time to operate their part-time business. Their dream of true financial independence is coming true because they did not let the "you don't have time" people destroy their goal.

As an aside, I am appalled at how much time and how much physical and moral damage is done by the relatively new American institution known as the "happy hour." Some people spend fifteen hours a week getting smashed and wasting time in bars. Just think what these people could do if they put those hours, and dollars, to a good purpose!

The I-lack-the-time dream destroyer is self-imposed. We tell ourselves we are too busy. Well, everyone lives exactly 1,440 minutes every 24 hours. Each of us decides whether to use our time productively or waste it.

*Dream Destroyer #6: But the economy is bad.* This is an old standby excuse for not starting a new venture, changing jobs, or making an investment. Most people use it, and most people suffer because they do. To be sure, a capitalistic economy has its ups and downs. There has never been a time when all stocks, bonds, real estate, or other investments all went up or down in price.

Look at it this way. The economy is always selectively good. There are always some excellent investments. But most investors don't understand this. Two mistakes they make are (1) they buy when everyone else is buying, and (2) they sell when everyone else is selling.

Only a minority of investors make a lot of money, because only a few have the stamina to avoid the herd instinct. Joseph Kennedy, father of President Kennedy, was a classic example. During the 1930's, when the nation's economy was in ruins, Mr. Kennedy increased his net worth more than 800 percent! Very simply, he knew that when people were frantically selling, that signaled a time to buy, and when they began to buy with undue enthusiasm, that was a time for him to sell.

Mr. Kennedy had deep-seated faith in our economic system. When the economy recovered—as it always does—he was ready.

If you are over age thirty, take a few minutes to review the economic performance of the people you knew well in high school. Chances are a few of them are on their way to financial independence. They're the ones who see the economy as always being selectively good. But most of your friends are probably just getting by. They're the ones who believe the awful headlines that tell people to surrender, give up, not take any risks, and be resigned that even worse economic times are a certainty.

Be a believer in the system or be a disbeliever. It's your choice. But keep this in mind. For decades, a few people have gotten rich by injecting economic fear into the minds of the masses.

For my part, I choose to side with the small minority who know the free world is on the threshold of a truly golden age.

## Five Steps for Creative Dreaming

Most people who dream don't really dream. They may have needs, wants, and desires, but they don't follow the dream procedures that work. Here they are:

*Step 1: Answer three basic questions about yourself.* A

wise old professor of mine at the University of Nebraska built an entire course in philosophy around having his students answer three critically important questions:

*(a) Who am I?* That is, what interests do I have? What special talents? What gives me the most joy? Answering the "who am I" question tells you what special assets and capabilities you have. I had a group of success-searching people answer this question recently, and the results were amazingly diverse. Some folks discovered they were loners and preferred to be around few other people. Others learned they were highly extroverted and needed to be with other people as much as possible. Some people learned that they preferred working with their hands. Others preferred working with their heads.

Each of us is unique. Knowing who you are is essential to answering the second question:

*(b) Where do I want to go?* An overwhelming majority of people you know have at best only a vague idea of why they are alive or where they are headed. If you want to have your eyes opened and learn the truth of this statement, do a little experiment. It's also a lot of fun. Here's the experiment:

Find a clipboard. This makes you look more official. Position yourself on a busy street and interview five people at random. Begin by asking, "Sir (or Madam), may I ask you a few questions?" They'll reply with something like, "Okay," or "Do you want to know who I'm going to vote for in the next election?"

Ask them this one question: "Why did you get up this morning?" Most of your respondents will look at you as if they think you're all the way out of it. So repeat the question, "Why did you get up this morning?"

Chances are the person will reply with, "Well, I had to go to work."

Then ask, "Why did you have to go to work?"

The respondent will likely reply with something like, "Well, I gotta eat."

Next, ask, "Why do you have to eat?" At this point, the other person will look at you as if you really are loco and say something like, "Well, so I can live."

Then as the real eye-opener, ask, "Why do you have to live?" The other person will think a second or two and then reply with, "So I can get up tomorrow morning and go to work."

The masses of people get up so they can go to work so they can earn a living so they can go to work so they can earn a living so they can go to work . . .

Doesn't that say something disturbing about society? Now success-oriented people get up in the morning so they can do something that carries them upward, not downward or sideways. They get up to enjoy life, meet interesting people, earn more money, do more with and for those they love, and help others to achieve.

It is extraordinarily important that we know where we want to go. Getting up for sixteen hours so we can afford to sleep eight hours is not the good life. Yet for tens of millions of people, that is their reason for being.

*(c) How do I get where I want to go?* Now I don't think you're like the people described in the street interview or you wouldn't be reading this book. Assuming you have a fix on where you want to go, the next question is, "How do I get there?" Each of us is unique and each of us has different goals. But there are three guidelines that, if followed, will propel us into the orbit we want.

First, get the best possible training and experience to qualify you for what you want to do. If you want to become a great salesperson, for example, get a job where you'll receive top-notch instruction and guided experience. Or if you want to become a computer expert, real-estate appraiser, or psychologist, affiliate with an organization where you will learn the ins and outs of your profession. Affiliate with a second-class organization and you'll learn second-class methods and procedures. (Later in the book, specific techniques are suggested for selecting a mentor—and everyone needs one.)

Second, be willing to sacrifice and then sacrifice some more. One thing all achievers have in common is the willingness to sacrifice in order to achieve goals. A friend of mine is a real-estate broker. One afternoon, he and I talked about how he got to the top of his profession.

"It wasn't easy," he explained, "but I did have sense enough early in my career to do what you suggested. I got a job with a very reputable real-estate firm, straight commission, of course. But the going was really tough. The first year I made in commissions just about a third what I would have earned in a corporate administrative job. But somehow, I was determined to hang on. I like real estate."

"Well, you certainly have it made now," I said. "What happened?"

"Oh, a lot more bitter times lay ahead," he replied. "I began to learn from my mistakes and I got some excellent coaching. And the commissions began to build fast. Then, almost suddenly, the real-estate market crashed. Because of high interest rates, lack of cash, and a fear psychology, my income dropped seventy-five percent. And it stayed down for three years. But during that time, while other agents dropped out of the business like flies, I kept working my clientele. I let them know I was trying my best to sell their properties.

"Finally, the recession ended and a real-estate boom developed and my sales skyrocketed. You see, by making a lot of sacrifices during the real-estate recession, I had earned very little money, but I created an enormous amount of what I call 'confidence capital.' The real-estate developers I had worked with when times were bad believed in me, and now I'm reaping the rewards. Last year I earned over two hundred thousand dollars in commissions."

Getting good advice and making sacrifices pay off.

*Step 2: Dream in specifics, not generalities.* Once we know who we are, where we want to go, and how to get there, the next step is to get specific about what we want. Typically, people state their dreams like this: "I'd like to make a lot of money," or "I'd like to have a better job," or "I'd like to have a business of my own and be my own boss." The problem with these dreams is that they are far too general. How much is "a lot of money"? What is a "better job"? Or what kind of "business" do you want?

People who phrase their dreams in specifics have an infinitely greater chance of reaching them than people who have only vague ideas of what they want. So, if you want to earn more money, state precisely how much you plan to earn and by what date. If your goal is a better job, write out a detailed description of the job you want. And if your dream is a business of your own, describe what kind of business it will be and when you will start it.

Most people are wishers. Be a creative dreamer instead—someone who knows what, precisely what, he or she wants.

*Step 3: Set a time frame for your dream fulfillment.* This dream-fulfillment requirement was suggested in Step 2. But let me elaborate just a bit. It is a fact that people work more efficiently and faster when they impose deadlines or a timetable on what they do. Some time ago, I knew two well-educated young men who had considerable expertise in computer-systems design. They decided they would open a consulting firm and sell their services to businesses too small to design their own systems. Every weekend for a year they planned their future business. They continued planning for a second year, and a third year. By this time, they finally concluded there was too much competition, so they'd better give up the idea of their own consulting firm.

Imagine how different the result would likely have been if they had agreed at the outset, "We'll spend our weekends planning for one year (or six months), and then we'll open our business."

Keep in mind that as Disraeli said, "Life is too short to be little." If you live until age 75, you will have spent only 27,391 days, 3,910 weeks, or 912 months on this earth. Life is too short to waste. Dreams are fulfilled only through action, not through endless planning to take action.

*Step 4: Visualize the dream as already attained.* A young friend of mine who held a beginning management job with an airline shared with me his dream and what he's doing to fulfill it.

"I know I'm going to make it into senior management in ten years. No one I know at my level is working harder or is smarter or has more desire than I to make it to the top. But I'm doing something else to make sure my wife and I and our two little kids enjoy the really good life."

"I'm curious," I said. "It seems like you're on the right track. But what else are you doing to achieve the good life?"

"I'll tell you," he replied. "My extra encouragement is to go a little out of the way once or twice a week on my way to work. I drive through an extra-fine residential area where the homes are large and custom-designed, where the lots are at least two acres, and the neighborhood is nearly perfect.

"Then I do something else," he added. "I ask myself,

how do these people afford to live in such beautiful, exclusive homes?"

"What kinds of answers do you get?" I asked.

"Well," my friend answered, "some of these people were born into wealth. But most of them, I've learned, made it on their own. Like you say, they had a big dream and made it come true. I've got a big dream, too, and I'm going to make it come true."

There are many ways to visualize a dream. If the dream is a specific income, paste the amount on the steering wheel of your car or on the bathroom mirror—any place that you'll be reminded of it several times a day. Or, when you're alone, say out loud—again, several times a day, "This year I will earn ———— dollars." Do these things and gradually your subconscious, that mysterious, all-powerful part of your mental apparatus, will guide you to your dream achievement.

*Step 5: Make a total commitment to your dream.* There is a psychological law, poorly understood and seldom applied, that says in effect that nothing can stop the totally committed individual from achieving carefully thought-out goals. Translated, this law means that if you are totally determined, willing to make all needed sacrifices, and keep your mind on winning the objective, you will achieve your goal.

Most of us have heard losing football coaches explain after the game, "I guess we weren't up [totally committed] to win today," or "Frankly, we weren't in condition today [the team didn't make the necessary sacrifices in training last week] to win."

Some feel the decisive battle of World War II was one in which the United States did not participate. That battle was the sinking of the German battleship *Bismarck.* The British naval commanders "knew" they could not sink this huge, new, all-powerful ship. But Prime Minister Churchill was totally committed. He issued the order, "Sink the *Bismarck.*" And the *Bismarck* was sunk.

Nothing, absolutely nothing, can stop the totally committed will.

## How to Profit Most from *The Magic of Getting What You Want*

Let me commend you for reading this chapter. It tells a lot about you. It says you're tired of less than the best—that you want more of the good things—more money, wealth, influence, and happiness. The fact that you're reading this book suggests that you want to move upward faster, with less wasted effort and fewer mistakes.

Those are great goals and very few people have them. Now, to maximize your experience using *The Magic of Getting What You Want,* follow these four suggestions.

1. Read the entire book as quickly as you can. Read it in two or three evenings or on a weekend. This will give you a feel for the philosophy of thinking more. It will serve as an overall orientation session to an old, yet brand-new concept for achievement and satisfaction. Immediately, as you read the principles and the examples that explain them, you will begin to see what differentiates the successful from the less-than-successful people.

2. Next, spend a week slowly and carefully rereading each chapter. Make notes. Underline concepts and guidelines that have special application to you.

3. Encourage others close to you, members of your family, your special friends, and perhaps your work associates to join you in discussing *The Magic of Getting What You Want.* You may want to spend an occasional evening or weekend holding a group discussion about the concepts presented.

4. Finally, and very important, apply the guidelines at

work, in the home, and in all social situations. See for yourself how they do work wonders in making for more successful living. Practice the guidelines until they become habits.

In a nutshell, put these concepts to work:

- Thinking more is your key to personal prosperity and enjoyment.
- Decide now to go for your own utopia and enjoy the best this life offers.
- Write your own obituary. See where the status quo will take you.
- Decide to scale up, not scale down.
- Solve budget problems by discovering how to earn more, not cut back.
- Avoid these Dream Destroyers:
  a) You don't have enough education.
  b) You lack capital.
  c) You've got to be "realistic."
  d) The field is overcrowded.
  e) You don't have the time.
  f) The economy is bad.
- Seek out Dream Builders. Avoid Dream Destroyers.
- Use these five keys for creative dreaming:
  a) Know who you are, where you want to go, and learn how to get where you want to go.
  b) Dream in specifics, not generalities.
  c) Set a deadline for dream fulfillment.
  d) Visualize the dream as already attained.
  e) Make a total commitment to your dream.

START THE DREAM PROCESS IN ACTION NOW!

# 2

# Look Again: You Can Make Yourself Even More A-OK

Years ago, I heard one child taunt another by saying, "I wish I could buy you for what you're worth and sell you for what you think you're worth. I'd make a fortune." It was another way of saying, "You're not as good or as smart as you think you are."

The remark, probably learned by the child from his parents, was not then and isn't now a nice comment—enough to destroy any thought of a better life.

From time to time I have reflected on that remark, but in a turned-around way. I wish I could "buy" other people for what they down deep think they are worth and sell them for what they potentially are worth. I'd make an enormous fortune.

Look at it this way. Most of the people you know suffer from self-depreciation, lack of confidence, and deep-seated feelings of inadequacy. They feel incompetent, insecure, and inept. Most people exercise little influence over their children, support personnel, and others they relate to. Self-depreciated people never control; instead, they allow themselves to be controlled by others, because fear is shaping their own destiny.

But people can, if they truly will, move up, out, and beyond those who try to hold them back.

## Be Certain of This: Your Self-image Is the Decisive Difference

Your self-image is a composite—a montage—of all the mental pictures you take of yourself—mind pictures of how you behave as a family person, what your fellow workers and associates think of you, your past successes and failures, the physical appearance you project, and what will happen to you if you take a certain action such as speaking up in public, tackling a new assignment, or joining a new group.

People with a positive self-image have these characteristics: They respect others and they respect themselves. They know they are good and getting even better. They play fair, and give all they've got to their families, their jobs, and their communities.

People with a positive self-image make good things happen. They work toward making life better, advancing technology, creating jobs, and helping others succeed. Those who develop a positive self-image are fun to be around, assume leadership positions, live well financially, and set a great example for others.

Folks with a negative self-image are convinced they are second-rate. They often harbor disrespect—even contempt—for themselves. They are afraid to stand up to the challenges of daily living and withdraw from helping others because they feel their efforts would probably be useless anyway.

The people who evaluate themselves negatively make up the masses of people who fail or, at best, live in mediocrity. They endure a lot of dissatisfaction, defeat, and discomfort, attract bad luck, know other people have it "in" for them, and regard their world as a prison they must live in until they die.

## Make Your Mentalvision Work for You, Not Hold You Back

All day long, people turn on one of their two private TV networks—I call it mentalvision—and watch mind movies of themselves in various situations. People everywhere, driving down the expressways, riding buses, trains, and planes—even in classrooms, sitting at a desk, or attending meetings—give surprisingly little attention to the physical reality around them. Instead, most of their concentration is devoted to watching mental movies on the self-depreciation network or the self-appreciation network.

## How Self-image Affects Romance

Some people depreciate themselves in everything they consider doing—even romance. A man may be attracted to a woman and want to date her. But his mentalvision tells him: She's too attractive for me, her education and family background are probably far superior to mine, and my friends will laugh at me if they find out I asked her to go out with me and she said no.

A self-depreciating woman may want to ask a man for a date, but when she turns on her mentalvision, she sees discouraging mind pictures: Women who ask men for dates are still ridiculed, I'm not attractive enough to interest him, he's got an important job and I'm only a secretary, and he's probably romantically involved with someone else.

In both of the above cases, the mentalvision programs sign off with "Forget it."

In placing a value on ourselves, consciously or subconsciously, we compare our strengths and weaknesses with other people and then arrive at a figure of how much we should earn, the standard of living we should be satisfied with, or how far up the ladder of life we should be able to climb.

And almost always people appraise themselves far below their real or true potential value.

About a year ago, the head of a medium-sized computer-software company related an experience that illustrates this point. "We needed a general administrative assistant," he explained. "We advertised the position extensively on a 'salary open' basis and got a lot of applications. Our choice finally narrowed down to two people. Both were about the same age and experience level. And both had similar career paths. On paper, two people, Mr. A and Mr. B, looked almost like identical twins.

"Which one did you pick and why?" I asked.

"Well, I chose Mr. B," the president replied. "As I mentioned, the salary was 'open.' When I asked Mr. A what compensation he expected, his voice changed, he crossed his legs, lost eye-contact with me, and almost in a whisper stated his figure, which was about what we thought the job was worth.

"That same day I discussed salary expectations with Mr. B. I asked him the same question I had asked Mr. A, 'What salary do you expect?' Mr. B looked me right in the eye. In a steady and direct voice, and without wavering one bit, he quoted a figure that was fifty percent higher than Mr. A had requested. I told B that another apparently equally qualified applicant would accept the job for considerably less.

"Then B said to me, 'I'm sure the other applicant you're considering would do a good job. But I feel I can do a great job. You see,' B continued, 'the tests you gave us and your checks of our references told you a lot about the other person and me. But I feel I have extraordinary initiative and enthusiasm—qualities that tests and reference checks don't really show. I think I'll prove to be worth every dollar you pay me, plus a lot more. I don't regard the salary I request as a cost—it's more like an investment in increased productivity.'

"Well," my friend went on, "applicant B sold me and we hired him. He simply had a higher regard for himself than applicant A."

"How's he working out?" I asked.

"Just wonderful," my friend responded. "His performance bears out what I've heard you say so often, 'People are worth pretty much what they think they're worth.'"

*Available on the Self-Depreciation Network*

| *Channels* | *Movies Showing Today* |
| --- | --- |
| Revenge Channel | —"Why and how you should get even with your superior or co-worker for the wrong he (she) has done you." |
| | —"How to put your mate back in her(his) place for not telling you the truth about spending so much money." |
| Fear of Failure Channel | —"You're a loser: It is foolish to try." |
| | —"Remember what happened before when you tried to make extra money?" |
| | —"Don't apply for the job, because you won't get it." |
| You Can't Prosper Channel | —"Five reasons why you should be content with mediocrity like everyone else." |
| | —"Facts that prove only people who cheat get rich." |
| | —"Why it is impossible to invest successfully." |
| You Don't Feel Good Channel | —"Three reasons why your headache means you're getting the flu." |
| | —"Understand why you feel worse as you grow older." |

*Viewing Results:* You feel terrible, fearful, and develop that I'm-a-loser-and-life-isn't-worth-living attitude. The trip toward mediocrity—then failure—is speeded up.

## Self-Appreciation Network

| *Channels* | *Movies Showing Today* |
|---|---|
| Join the Winners Channel | —"Three reasons why you'll get what you want today."<br>—"Try twice as hard and earn five times as much."<br>—"Set a big goal—then double it! Here's how." |
| Make Someone Happy Today Channel | —"Doing good for others is being good to yourself."<br>—"Volunteer to share."<br>—"Congratulate people and enjoy life more." |
| You've Got What It Takes Channel | —"You're twice as smart as you think! Here's proof!"<br>—"You have no real liabilities or shortcomings."<br>—"You are unique—you can be a champion." |
| Count Your Blessings Channel | —"Your family, friends, and co-workers need you—help them."<br>—"Discover the real promise in your job." |

---

*Viewing Results:* Success is made easier. Living is more challenging, more fun. You begin galloping toward everything superior—better job, more love, more money, and more old-fashioned satisfaction.

## How Elaine Discovered She Was A-OK at Age Forty-five

I met Elaine W. two months ago at an awards banquet for top sales and management people in a direct-to-the-consumer cosmetics company. Elaine was there because she was going to receive an award for her outstanding performance for the year just ended. I was going to speak to the group after the awards presentation. Elaine and I happened to be seated beside each other. Almost immediately, we got to talking about a subject of mutual interest—why do so few succeed and so many self-destruct in this world of plenty? Why do the majority just get by spiritually and financially? Why do so many people lead such dull, monotonous, unrewarding lives?

During the twenty minutes or so we had between salad and dessert, Elaine told me how she became a happy, prosperous, and greatly admired person.

"When I was forty-five," she explained, "our youngest child went off to college. My husband traveled a lot, and soon I was bored silly—even despondent at times. Until then, my life had been devoted to rearing three kids. The job skills I learned," she laughed, "were changing diapers, washing clothes, feeding and caring for children, and chauffeuring them to and from school. Our social life wasn't much. Once in a while I'd help entertain my husband's business associates, but that was about it."

"Well," I commented, "something must have happened. I know you're going to get the top award tonight."

"I decided I'd get a job," Elaine explained. "My husband urged me not to, because he had a fine position with an electronics firm. But I told him I needed work for therapeutic reasons. So I started job hunting. I found trying to get a job with no track record to be a challenge!

I had not gone to college, and the jobs I wanted required a knowledge of word processing, editing, typing, managing, or some other skill I didn't have.

"During the first month of job hunting, I had not received even one offer. At noon one day after three disappointing interviews that morning, I stopped at a motel restaurant for lunch. My waiter sensed my dejection and asked what was troubling me. I mentioned that I was having a tough time finding a job. He looked me over carefully and then said, 'Look, I'm the assistant manager of this restaurant. Why don't we talk? We like to hire middle-aged women as waitresses and hostesses. They're much more dependable than young women and much less distracting.'"

Elaine, with a little fire in her eyes, continued, "Now I might have considered his offer, but when he told me I was 'middle-aged' and no longer attracted men's attention, I gulped my food and left as fast as I could.

"Then, walking through the lobby, a strange thing happened. I noticed a sign that said, 'Free Seminar on Making Money in Cosmetics, two P.M. in the Randolph Room.' Well, it was almost two, so I thought: Why not take a look? After all, I had nothing to lose."

"So, that's how you got into the cosmetics business," I commented.

"Yes. In the next sixty minutes, I became convinced I could sell cosmetics to my friends and friends of my friends. Soon I was bringing other women into the business and moving up in the organization. That happened seven years ago, and I've enjoyed every minute. My income is in the top two percent in the company and, more importantly, I enjoy this business."

"I'll bet your husband and children are really pleased with your success," I remarked.

Then, with tears in her eyes, Elaine told me that her

husband had died unexpectedly two years ago. She went on to explain that because of inflation, her husband's insurance would not have been adequate for her support. But her success in cosmetics had assured her an excellent standard of living, and a profit-sharing plan would help to cover her retirement someday.

"The kids," she smiled, "had been concerned about how I'd face life alone. Now they are satisfied Mom is A-OK.

"But perhaps the most important part of my success is what it has done for me spiritually," Elaine continued. "You see, no job on earth is as important as being a homemaker, but after twenty-five years of it I began to think that's all I could do—that I could never make it doing anything else. Now I've proved I can, and my self-esteem is tremendous! I like *me* and I am thrilled about how I am helping other women discover that they, too, are a whole lot better than they think."

Elaine's experience teaches us three big lessons:

1. We are never too old to start something new and succeed. Without advanced education and no specific job skills, Elaine is enjoying her success. Anyone can if they are committed.

2. Children want to see their parents find A-OK status. Most would rather see their parents enjoy some gainful experience than do nothing. Children want to watch their parents succeed, not just grow older and wait to die.

3. Nothing builds a positive self-image like success. So get in gear and start winning!

## For the Best Mentalvision, Keep on Selling Yourself to Yourself

Of all the mail I've received about *The Magic of Thinking Big*, the one topic most often commented on is "Prepare Your Own Sixty-Second Commercial." In a nutshell, the idea behind your own 60-second commercial is to put down in about 125 words why you are destined for greater success. Examples of points to develop are your exceptional initiative, integrity, attractiveness, liking of other people, willingness to sacrifice, and eagerness to accept responsibility.

Every letter I have received about my Sell Yourself to Yourself commercial was positive except one. A fellow in Iowa really tore the idea apart. He let me know that it was about the stupidest idea he had ever heard.

I answered this person by telling him, "I'm disappointed that you're displeased with the Sell Yourself to Yourself commercial." I ended my reply by asking him to do me a favor. "Just try it," I urged, "you're probably a very open-minded person and are willing to experiment with a concept before you reject it."

A few months later, I received this note from my doubting friend:

> Dear Dr. Schwartz:
>     You may remember me. I'm the guy who blasted your sixty-second commercial idea. Well, at your suggestion, I gave it a try. I "knew" it wouldn't work, but I confess it really does! My job performance is way up. I'm enjoying my life a lot more and I see a great future ahead.
>                                             Thanks again,
>                                             Walt B.

The point is simple: Constantly reminding yourself that you really are A-OK will make you even more successful; but dwelling on your limitations leads straight down the road to mediocrity and failure.

## Try Putting Your Commercial on Cassette

A growing number of people tell me how they have adapted the sixty-second written commercial concept to a spoken-word format. Some folks have expanded the sixty seconds to two or three minutes or even longer. What these people do is put their Sell Yourself to Yourself commercial on cassette tape. Then they listen to it at least once a day.

The people who have told me about their cassette-tape commercials do their "self ads" by themselves. But last month, Mary and Hank P. of Los Angeles, both of whom have good jobs and a promising sideline business, told me of their novel approach to making the "self sale."

"We do our commercial together," Mary explained. "On the same tape, Henry and I describe our assets, the promises of the future, our joy in being responsible for two great children, our goals and what, specifically, we are doing to achieve them, our recent accomplishments—those sorts of things."

"When do you play it?" I asked.

"We drive to work together every morning, and that's the first thing we do after starting the car. We often play it on the way home, too. We feel two simple secrets to having a great day are eating a good breakfast (for our bodies) and listening to our tape (for our minds)."

Then I asked whether they ever revise their tapes. "Oh, yes!" Henry replied. "We find that about every month we profit by doing a new tape. It covers the same selling points but in a little different way—that's good for reinforcement. It also gives an opportunity to add new reasons why we should be proud of ourselves."

Isn't your own commercial selling you to yourself a wonderful way to keep on thinking "I really am A-OK"?

## Try the Ultimate: Do Your Own TV Commercial Selling Yourself to Yourself

Let me tell you about another couple, Jane and Harold B., whom I met about a year ago who have carried the original sixty-second written commercial, "Sell Yourself to Yourself," from the audio-cassette stage all the way to television. They developed their own Sell Yourself to Yourself video cassette. Jane and Harold use their own TV camera to make commercials of themselves that they can play back on their TV set. Now, they can both see and hear themselves, making the impact even greater.

Jane told me that, besides making them aware of their assets and goals, films also show ways they can improve their posture, gestures, and body language in general. She also says that it helps them dress better and, in the process, helps them gain even more confidence.

When Jane and Harold told me about their self-sell commercials, I became so interested I asked them if they would send me details of how their "build yourself up" system works.

In a couple of weeks, I received a long letter from Jane. In part, she wrote:

"Our own commercial selling us to ourselves has had such a dramatic affect on our lives, we decided to broaden the use of this technique. We divided our lives into five key component parts. Then, for each part, we've made a three-minute 'commercial' or mini-program to reinforce what we believe in and what we should do to strengthen our commitment to those beliefs."

In her letter, Jane also described briefly the component parts of their life and outlined what she and Harold say and do on the TV tapes to live up to their highest standards. Briefly, here are the tape titles and their contents.

*Home Video Commercial #1: "Keep the Faith."* "This three-minute tape reminds us to remember God, His holy truth, and give thanks for the good things we enjoy. We also have segments on living by the Golden Rule, keeping the Commandments, and striving to try harder in reaching our goals."

*Home Video Commercial #2: "Totally Committed to Each Other."* Jane describes the contents of this tape as "expressing our love to each other, in heart, mind, body, and soul. On this tape, we also ask forgiveness from each other for those little temper losses and oversights that are part of the best marriages. This commercial really helps keep us solidly sold on each other. Also, we each give the reasons why we love each other."

*Home Video Commercial #3: "Make a 100 Percent Commitment to Our Children."* Jane and Harold have three children. Jane explains, "Our kids really are the center of our lives. We made this tape to remind us that our biggest responsibility is to love them, care for their spiritual and bodily needs, direct them, encourage them—let them know they are fine young people who can achieve goals—and spend time with them."

*Home Video Commercial #4: "Increase Income 20 Percent Per Year."* "Our financial goal is to increase our income at least twenty percent per year, so we made this video tape to burn that objective into our subconscious minds," Jane wrote. "Harold has a good job with the electric utility company, but our income-expansion plans focus on our own business we started two years ago. This tape reminds us of the specific steps we must follow to make our business grow—show our part-time business to other people, put at least ten hours a week into building the business, make at least one phone call per week to our distributors, and keep our customers satisfied."

*Home Video Commercial #5: "Share the Good Life."* "We learned," Jane explained, "that sharing is a cornerstone of success in all facets of life. This commercial shows how sharing ideas, plans, encouragement, and our good fortune helps others, and in the process helps us, too. Thanks to this tape, we're able to resist the terrible—and stupid—temptation to think selfishly."

After digesting Jane's description of their own TV self-advancement series, I phoned her to learn still more about how their system works.

"How often do you play them?" I asked.

"At least once a week," Jane replied. "We plan to remake each tape every three months to keep our advice to ourselves fresh."

"Do you have other ideas for using video tapes in your success program?" I inquired.

"We sure do!" Jane exclaimed. "We're going to help our children make their tapes to give them more strength and confidence. One tape they're planning is 'How to Get the Most Out of School.' Another is 'Secrets for Making Good Friends.' And we're encouraging all of our part-time business associates to make their own 'Sell Yourself to Yourself' commercials."

Then I asked, "Jane, do you let other people watch your commercials?"

"No," responded Jane. "You see, much of the power of our commercials is that they are tailored to our specific circumstances. Parts of them are very personal, very private. We encourage our friends to do what we did—develop tapes that apply directly to their lives."

Jane and Harold use words like "unbelievable," "fantastic," and "tremendous" to describe what doing commercials on how to do better in each major life component has done for them.

Truly, they are on the right track to getting the most out of life. Maybe you do not have the equipment to make your own TV commercials to help guide you. But you do have a pencil and paper. Try Jane and Harold's method and feel wonderful things happen.

Making films to remind yourself you're great and growing even greater is a wonderful approach to success. You are likely to see it grow in use rapidly.

## How to Turn a Loser into a Winner

Tim O., a branch sales manager for a company that sells fork-lift trucks, heard me speak recently at a meeting for marketing managers. Repeatedly, I drove home the point that no one has liabilities. People have only assets, some of which are better developed than others, but assets nevertheless.

I used many examples to make my point: a man who can't walk and heads a major company, individuals who never attended college who direct huge organizations, blind people who are in the precious-metals business, and folks who didn't really get started until they were past age sixty.

After the presentation, the sales manager approached me and said, "I really enjoyed your presentation. It was very well targeted to the situations I face every day. But there is one point you emphasized this afternoon that I can't buy."

"What's that?" I asked.

"Well," Tim replied, "you said that anyone, regardless of his or her job, has only assets, not liabilities."

"You're right," I agreed. "That's what I said because

that's what I've observed to be absolutely true. Whether we think something is good (an asset) or bad (a liability) depends strictly on the way we view the situation. Some people see only lemons, while other people see lemonade. One investor sees only useless land, while another sees an office complex on the land."

"Well, I don't agree," said Tim. "I'm about ready to terminate one of our salespeople. He's simply a bundle of liabilities. The guy does a lousy job of prospecting and he doesn't know how to close. I had a long talk with him yesterday. I was going to fire him tomorrow, but now you've confused me and I don't like being confused."

I paused for a few seconds and said, "Tim, tell me about the conversation you had with your salesman yesterday."

Tim replied, "I'm one of those up-front types. I told him he was doing an awful job of closing, and he's losing money for the company. In a nutshell, I told him to either shape up or ship out."

Then I said, "Tim, may I make a suggestion?"

"I wish you would," Tim said, "I came to this seminar for ideas to help me become a better manager."

"Fine," I replied. "Here is what I recommend. Tomorrow, spend a few minutes with John and apologize for your abrupt behavior of yesterday. Simply say, 'John, I'm sorry for coming down so heavily on you this week. I was stupid for calling you a poor closer. I know you've got a beautiful wife. Getting such a fine, beautiful, intelligent woman to marry you proves you're a great closer.' Build his ego, remind him of his strengths, and then give him the technical closing advice you feel he needs. Do these things, and John may just turn it all around."

Two months after this discussion, I got a call from Tim. He said, "I've got some good news that may interest you. I did what you said, built up John's ego; made him think like a winner. Last month he was third of fifteen salespeople in sales volume. This guy *is* turning out to be a winner."

Tim continued, "And even more important, in my overall plan I'm doing more to get the rest of the salespeople sold on themselves. And it's working."

A lot of people who work with us seem to be losers today. Every day some people are being told something like, "Sorry, your services are no longer needed. Your work hasn't met our expectations," or "Mary, this is a team effort and you're just not playing your position. Now I must tell you that effective the thirtieth of the month, you are terminated. You will, of course, get the usual one month's severance pay."

I've observed this about worker termination. When employees are dismissed because the company fails or because there is a severe production cutback, workers certainly aren't happy. But what personal self-esteem they have remains pretty much intact. After all, it was not their personal behavior that resulted in dismissal. But when people are fired because of their own bad performance, their egos are wounded. They usually feel a great deal of personal hurt and self-resentment. After all, when you dismiss an employee for ineffective performance, you're telling him or her to go home to wife or husband and the kids with the feeling "I couldn't cut it." And the embarrassment of forced termination makes one feel second-class around one's friends.

The point: Double your efforts to help your people feel they are special, important, potentially successful. Do this and watch them multiply their efforts to do more and do it better.

## Please Note: Nobody Moves Up by Being Put Down

To win influence over people, to get them to support you enthusiastically, and to cause them to cooperate with you, build them up, don't tear them down.

There is no evidence, absolutely none, from psychology, psychiatry, or any other source, that people are made more productive, happier, or better in any respect by being put down, embarrassed, threatened, or humiliated.

Yet in our environment we see many people trying to influence others by scolding, not showing them, by suppressing, not praising them. We see office managers berate typists, shop foremen yell at employees, teachers tell students they are stupid, and parents swear at their kids for minor infractions.

Then the office managers are surprised when typists make costly blunders, foremen cannot understand high employee turnover, teachers don't know why student performance is low, and parents are shocked when their kids run away, get hooked on drugs, or get into trouble.

Now, in any well-run organization, all people are important and they are created equal. And in the eyes of the smart manager, all members of the department are important, regardless of the tasks they perform. They simply play different positions on the team.

United Technologies Corporation made an excellent statement that shows the respect "little people"—in this case, secretaries—deserve.

LET'S GET RID
OF "THE GIRL"

Take one giant step forward for womankind and get rid of "the girl."

Your attorney says, "If I'm not here, just leave it with the girl."

The purchasing agent says, "Drop off your bid with the girl."

A manager says, "My girl will get back to your girl."

What girl?

Do they mean Miss Rose?

Do they mean Ms. Torres?

Do they mean Mrs. McCullough?

Do they mean Joy Jackson?

"The girl" is certainly a woman when she's out of her teens.

Like you, she has a name. Use it.

*Courtesy of United Technologies Corporation.*

Here is a good rule to follow: Develop the habit of making people feel more important. Show respect for the salesperson behind the counter and observe the difference in the way your package is wrapped; show a little kindness to the receptionist and notice how pleasant she is when she announces you; be polite to the waitress and enjoy better service; say something nice to the room clerk and your wake-up call will come through.

In a very real sense, your success is in the hands of others. Treat them like big, important, necessary individuals and you'll make life more profitable for yourself.

## How to Prevent Self-Depreciators from Corrupting You

People who make a commitment to use their mentalvision to see themselves in a positive light often ask how they can deal with self-depreciators in work situations, at home, and in their social lives. Dealing with self-depreciators is a real challenge because, if their influence rubs off on you, your chances for more money, promotions, and happiness are diminished.

Here are three types of self-depreciators and how you can handle them.

*(1) The Belittler* is a person who wants to put you down. Belittlers are self-depreciators who take devilish delight in putting you down, belittling what you do, achieve, and attain.

Consider these examples:

| *Situation* | *The Self-Depreciating Belittler* |
| --- | --- |
| 1. You start a business of your own and make money. | "He was just lucky. By accident he got into the business at the right time." |
| 2. You win a promotion. | "Anyone would get promoted if he polished the apple like he does." |
| 3. Your teenager wins a scholarship. | "You must have some real strong pull with the college trustees." |
| 4. You wear some new clothes to work. | "I saw that same suit (dress) advertised on sale at ———." (the cheapest store in town) |
| 5. You move into a finer home. | "In five years, the real-estate taxes will double." |

Belittlers, the put-you-downers, are found everywhere. They spend a great deal of mental energy trying to make you feel bad and look like nothing. Worse still, they try to get others to join them in their crusade to make you feel small.

Why? What is Mr. Belittler's problem? Simply this: The put-others-down folks suffer from self-depreciation. Their image of themselves is negative and small. Belittlers don't like themselves. They feel if they can attribute your successes to luck or pull, they will look bigger and better. By making fun of your awards, income, fine home, intelligent children, and promotions—your victories in life—they think they make themselves look bigger and better. It makes them feel better when they can reduce you to their petty level.

Belittlers are as stupid as a neighbor who breaks a window in your home thinking it will make her house look better. I once knew a belittler who paid his son to decorate the neighbors' trees with bathroom tissue! How foolish, and how damaging to the child's sense of right and wrong.

The belittlers are all around us. So how do we deal with them? Three suggestions:

First, feel sorry for them. They're sick. No one is born with a put-others-down mentality. They acquired the belittler philosophy from bad examples at home, at school, and from their peer groups.

Second, understand their problems, and try to ignore them. Remember, if the belittler can make you feel bad, if he can reduce you to his level, he has achieved his goal. Don't give him the satisfaction.

Third, avoid the temptation to "get even," "fight back," and "put the belittler in his place." You always lose when you try to set things straight with self-depreciating belittlers.

*(2) The Foul-Language Communicator.* Here's a clue to the way people think: The more a person engages in self-depreciation, the more likely that person uses filthy, putrid language. You see, self-depreciators think using repulsive, vulgar expletives and disgusting, negative words gives them status, makes them feel important, and proves they are big, brave, worldly people.

Unfortunately, people with the most despicable vocabularies often have a strong influence on peers, employees, and children. So the latter groups also begin using vile language.

How does one deal with foul-language communicators?

One of my friends, who runs a bakery, told me recently, "You know, I can't think of one person I have ever promoted because of foul language. But I can think of a number of people I did not promote because their choice of four-letter words and filthy language turned me off."

Avoid the language of self-depreciators. If you want to use four-letter words, there are many you can choose— words like good, kind, love, nice, pure, help, more, fine—and make your language reflect the real you, the self-confident optimist, not a self-depreciated fool.

The point is this: So-called "colorful" language indicates that its user is insecure and doesn't like himself. And those of us who want more by being really A-OK know that using foul language will never help us win the rewards we seek. But employing the negative words can, in fact, hold us back.

*(3) The Self-Depreciator Who Escapes Through Alcohol.* Many theories are advanced to tell us why some people let booze control their lives. It's been theorized that some people inherit a tendency to drink. Another equally misleading theory is that some people's metabo-

lism demands it. The plain truth is that the main reason for alcohol dependency is insecurity, a word that means fear of self, fear of others, fear of one's work, inability to cope with the realities of life.

Alcohol-dependent people affect all of us directly and indirectly. About the only way you can help anyone with this problem is to do all you can to make the person feel needed, wanted, and important. The only real cure is to help the affected individual develop a deep sense of self-worth.

If that doesn't work, and unfortunately it may not if the problem is deeply entrenched, make sure the person does as little harm to others as possible. Bad as it may be, it is better to remove yourself and your children from a self-hating, excessive drinker who won't adopt the cure (self-worth) than to endanger the emotional, physical, and financial well-being of yourself and those close to you.

In a capsule, make yourself more A-OK. Here's how:

- Accept the fact that you're better than you think.
- Recognize that your image of you determines how far you will go in earning money, friends, and influence.
- Practice positive mentalvision. See yourself in successful situations. See what can be, not only what is.
- Put self-appreciation to work. Keep on selling yourself to yourself.
- Remember, nobody moves up by being put down. So build people up and win your goals.
- Don't let belittlers put you down. Feel sorry for them instead. Never fight back or try to get even.
- Keep in mind that foul language suggests a lack of self-confidence. Using it never helps one get ahead.

# 3

# How to Get Others to Help You Win!

Winning means many wonderful, positive things. Winning means achieving great goals, getting the job you really want, overcoming impossible obstacles. Winning means achieving superior status, influencing others to act, and scoring big in the game of life.

Simply stated, winning means success.

Losing is the opposite of winning. Losing means negative, terrible things. Losing means getting kicked around at work, not having enough money, and having to go second-class. Losing means disgrace, disappointment, and disgust.

Simply stated, losing means failure.

An amazing fact in this age of plenty is that most people are losers. The majority of people are unhappy with their income, lead dull lives, and are chronically sick with various ailments. They live life as if it is a sentence in a prison called Earth.

Now the good news is that none of us has to be a loser. Anyone who puts forth intelligent effort can win, and win big.

The statement that follows should be read twice before you continue: Your success is determined not by what you do, but rather by what you cause other people to do.

I'm going to repeat that statement again so you will be

sure to read it twice: Your success is determined not by what you do, but rather by what you cause other people to do.

## Let Other People Do the Work, You Be the Coach

Moses was one of the earliest teachers to learn that he could accomplish more simply by letting others help him. When Moses was leading the Israelites to the Promised Land, his father-in-law, Jethro, noticed that Moses was overworked, and if he continued at that pace, the people would soon suffer.

So Jethro solved Moses' problem. He told Moses to divide his people into groups of one thousand, then divide the thousands into groups of one hundred, then the groups of one hundred into two groups of fifty people each. Next, to divide the groups of fifty into five groups of ten.

Then Jethro told Moses to tell the leaders of each group to go to the next-highest level with any problems they couldn't solve. Moses was also advised to instruct the leaders of the thousand-person groups to bring to him only those problems that they could not solve.

By following Jethro's advice, Moses was able to devote his time to the truly important problems—the ones that only he had the ability to handle.

In a nutshell, Jethro taught Moses to delegate. He said, in effect, "All work should be performed at the lowest level of competence."

*Delegating is the key to getting others to help you achieve more of what you want.* A manager in a paint-manufacturing company explained delegation in this way: "Letting lower-level people handle problems makes sense because of the two 'M's."

"What do you mean?" I asked.

"Well," my friend continued, "the first M stands for Money. From the standpoint of money, all work in the company should be performed at the lowest level of competence.

"It makes no economic sense whatsoever for a person who makes forty dollars an hour to do work that a ten-dollar-an-hour person can do as well, or possibly better. I believe that *not* delegating work is the biggest financial waste possible in business. And people who insist on doing everything themselves never rise very high in an organization."

"What's the second M stand for?" I asked.

"That stands for Motivation. A lot of managers don't realize this, but many support-people want to do work delegated from upper levels. It's flattering. It makes them feel more useful, more needed. Delegation is also a good way to test an individual to see what level of work he or she is able to do.

"As a senior manager, I have learned I can delegate to others many of the things I had been doing myself for years: telephone calls, arrangement of meetings, letter writing, out-of-town travel reservations, greeting visitors, and reading reports."

Delegation can also help you in your relationships with people. I remember, as a youngster, going to a country school where all eight grades sat in the same room. It was considered an honor to be asked to dust erasers, bring the teacher a glass of water, or empty the pencil sharpener.

In family situations, children will want to do chores if their parents show appreciation and let them know they play a key role in the family unit.

Delegate; share your work load and you'll get the job done more economically and make people feel more important at the same time.

## The "You Are the Potter, They Are the Clay" Philosophy Works Miracles

Let me share with you a conversation I had with Leonard S. on a flight from New York to St. Louis some time ago. It explains an infallible method for getting others to help you gain more of what you want.

As Leonard and I talked, I learned that he was part-owner and president of a plastics company. I asked if he had always been in the plastics business, and he said he had not. He went on to explain that his first ten years after graduating from college had been spent as a high school football coach.

I asked him, "Were you a pretty good coach?"

He replied, "Actually, until the last game of my first year, I was a terrible coach. We won that game, but by only one point. After that, I was terrific. My teams won the state championship four times in my ten years of coaching. All totaled, we won eighty-two percent of the games played."

"That's quite a record," I replied, "but I'm a little curious. What happened to make the last game in that first year a turning point for you and your career as a coach?"

"Well," Leonard explained, "the Sunday before the season's final game, my minister preached a very practical sermon based on the concept, 'You are the potter, and your people are the clay.' As he spoke, the solution to my problem hit me. My team was losing not because of their inability, but because of my thinking. For the first time I was able to see that, in my relationship to the team, I was the potter and they were the clay.

"After lunch that Sunday," Leonard continued, "I did some serious thinking about it. I concluded that the fundamental reason the team was losing was my own negative and passive thinking."

He leaned forward as he explained, "You see, I knew

the school had a losing tradition over the years. I had accepted that. We were expected to lose. And I knew most of my players were relatively small of stature. I knew, too, that none of them had had much experience, since they were mostly freshmen and sophomores. I knew all the negatives. I had rationalized everything so that one win out of a whole year was no big deal. The team, the clay if you will, sensed how I felt and performed accordingly. My thinking had become their thinking. They, too, had accepted defeat as the status quo. They expected to lose, and so they did lose."

"What did you do after you made this discovery?" I asked.

"I'll tell you what I did," Leonard went on. "I made up my mind that we were going to win that last game, that's what. I was aware, of course, that the opposing team was favored by at least twenty-eight points—they hadn't been beaten all season. Despite the odds, I convinced myself we were going to win. The next thing I knew I had to do was turn my team's thinking from 'We are going to lose' to 'We are going to win.'"

"How did you manage that?" I asked. "You probably didn't have much time to prepare. Less than a week, wasn't it?"

"Yes," Leonard replied. "Late that Sunday afternoon, I phoned each player and told him we were going to pull off the biggest upset in the school's history at that game on Friday evening. I said to the members of the team, 'Make no mistake about it, we will win!'

"At Monday's practice session, I gathered the team together out on the field and said, 'Today we will have no physical drills, only mental drills.' Then I instructed them to shout in unison just before every scrimmage, 'We will win!', and after each huddle to slap another player's hand and shout, 'Win!'

"All that week, the team thought 'Win,' and the

cheerleaders picked up the idea, too. Before every offensive play, they got the crowd to shout, 'Win offensive,' and before every defensive play everyone shouted, 'Win defensive.' The players loved the concept. By Friday night, those kids were really hyper. The rest is history. They beat that number-one team."

"It sounds like changing your attitude made a lot of difference," I observed.

"No, not a lot of difference," he said, "It made *all* the difference. In fact, one hundred percent of the difference. When I discovered that I was the potter and they were the clay, I knew the secret of success. I knew that my thinking had to shape their thinking."

"Leonard," I said. "I'm really curious. Why did you change careers at a time when you were so obviously experiencing success?"

"Though I was a success on the football field and enjoyed what I was doing, I wondered if I could be a success in the business world, too. The chance came along to join my company thirteen years ago as part of its sales team. Two months after I took the job, however, the company filed for bankruptcy.

"Although I hadn't been with the company very long, it was long enough to realize that the basic cause of the bankruptcy was the unbelievably negative attitude I'd observed in the senior managers. They, of course, placed the blame on unfair competition, the bad state of the economy, excessive government regulation, and so forth. In fact, they placed the blame everywhere but in the right place—on themselves," Leonard explained.

"Well, to shorten a long story," he continued, "I talked with a number of friends I'd made while coaching, and we put together enough money to buy the company. Because of the bankruptcy factor, we were able to buy it at a fraction of its real value. Then my friends told me to go ahead and run it and make money."

"And how have you done in the plastics business?" I asked.

"Great," Leonard replied. "We're expanding to new products all the time, and for five years in a row we've increased profits by twenty percent or more each and every year."

"Apparently, you put the 'We will win' philosophy to work in your business venture, too," I commented.

"Exactly," he replied. "When I was made president after the reorganization, I immediately removed the negative personnel and began to instill in the minds of everyone, from the sweeper to our top personnel, the idea that we will win, we will increase efficiency, we will reduce waste, and we will sell more. It's paid off."

Take note: Leonard (a) saw himself as the potter, the person fully in charge, (b) realized his thinking shaped the thinking of his support personnel, and (c) adopted an absolute "We will win" philosophy. The result: Leonard is a winner.

Remember, people who fail think losing; people who win think winning. This is a law that cannot be repealed.

## Whatever Seeds Parents Sow, They Later Reap

For many of us, the biggest example-setting role we play is that of parent. And some parents do a very bad job. Let me tell you about an eye-opening discussion I had a year ago with Dr. Wanda B., a psychologist who specializes in providing counsel to teenagers between the ages of thirteen and sixteen.

Wanda told me that most of the young people she

counsels come from upper-middle-income homes. She also said that most of them suffer pretty much the same problem, though with different symptoms. She describes the problem simply as the parental bad-example syndrome.

"Parents seek my help because their children are smoking, sniffing, shooting drugs, and drinking; because they're doing poorly in school, staying out late at night, becoming dangerously active sexually, having run-ins with police, and even threatening suicide," Wanda explained. "Even though they come from affluent families, the young people I treat have serious problems.

"Affluence is no protection against teenage problems," she went on. "In fact, in some homes it is a contributing factor."

I thought I had a pretty good idea of what Wanda meant by "the parental bad-example" syndrome, but I asked her to explain it nevertheless.

"The syndrome is basically this: The youngsters are simply acting out the roles they've seen their parents play over the years. Most of my young patients have parents who drink, often to excess. However, when the children get high on booze or drugs, the parents get angry.

"Many children see their parents quarrel, hear them make petty remarks about other people, boast when they can avoid paying taxes, complain about minor illnesses, break traffic laws, speak disparagingly of those in authority, use bad language as a matter of course, even flirt with someone else's spouse."

"Sounds to me as though the parents are the ones who need help," I observed.

"I agree," Wanda replied. "But they should have had help before they became parents.

"Look," she continued, "let's face it. A child models his or her behavior on the behavior of the parents. By the time I see these teenagers, it's next to impossible in many instances to bring about corrective action.

"I've reached one big conclusion in my work," Wanda continued. "If all parents did their very best to set good examples, my services wouldn't be needed."

"What about peer pressure?" I asked. "Many parents believe that their children's problems come from hanging around with people their own age who have been brought up with wrong ideals and values."

"The influence of companions is a factor," Wanda replied, "but the real source of the problem is the parents. Many young people are tempted to misbehave by peers, but few will succumb to the temptation unless they have first observed their parents behaving badly."

Wanda gazed into the distance, commenting with a hint of sadness, "The most important influence on a child is the parents. How I wish, desperately so, that parents everywhere would recognize that it is their example, their attitudes, that must ultimately shape, often forever, the attitudes and performance of their children."

## How a Miracle Happened When a Parent Took Responsibility

A few months ago, I had some business to transact in a small county seat. While there, I decided to visit an old friend who had served as a judge for twenty-five years. Now in his seventies, he continues to practice law in a small way in order, as he puts it, "to keep thinking young."

During the last ten years of my friend's judgeship, he had presided over more than two hundred drug cases. He began reminiscing about hearing those cases, most of which involved young people.

"What stands out in your memory of dealing with those teenagers?" I asked. "What was the most important lesson you learned about young people?"

"Well, if you're asking me what I learned about kids I didn't know already, I'd have to say very little. Many young people want to do what they see their parents do, but which they've been told not to do. And most of them want to sow wild oats," he replied. "This generation of young people simply doesn't buy logic such as, 'Do as I say, not as I do,' or 'You're not old enough for that,'" the judge continued.

"But," he added, "if you're asking me what I learned about the parents of those young people, I'd have to say a great deal."

"I'm curious," I injected. "Would you explain what you mean?"

"Simply this," my friend continued. "The vast majority of parents do not accept what I consider to be an indisputable fact—that they are responsible for the misdeeds of their kids."

"I agree, but I'm sure a lot of people would take issue with us on that point," I commented. "Explain how you reached your conclusion."

"Generally, I divide the parents of the drug violators into three categories. The first are from poor economic backgrounds. Often these parents wouldn't even attend the court proceedings. When they did, and when the youngster was sentenced, I might hear a parent say, 'You got just what you deserved,' or 'I hope they straighten you out,' as though spending months, or maybe even years, with veteran criminals would straighten anybody out.

"In my experience," he went on, "I also served for seven years on the state parole board. I can assure you, if a young offender is not a criminal when he goes to prison, he certainly is by the time he comes out.

"The second group of parents, the ones in the middle-income bracket, usually show up in court. Those parents often blame their child's peers, the schools, movies, television, and, in fact, anything and everything other than themselves. Even before they leave the courtroom, you can hear comments directed at their child such as, 'Haven't you embarrassed us enough?,' and 'Don't ever get in trouble again,' and 'Next time this happens, don't come to us for help.'"

"And the third group of parents?" I asked.

"The third group represents the well-to-do, the affluent sector. They, of course, would retain the best legal counsel and employ all sorts of gimmicks to try to get the case dismissed. But like the other two groups, they, too, would refuse to accept responsibility for their children's actions. Many blamed what they called the stupid laws, the idiot police, and the unfair judicial system. In fact, in my many years of service as a judge, I had only one case in which a parent took full responsibility for his son's behavior."

"Tell me about that one," I requested.

"The facts in the case were clear-cut, as I recall," he explained. "The boy, barely sixteen years old, had been picked up with several ounces of marijuana. It was enough to commit him under the statutes. At that particular time, judges were under enormous pressure to send the violators to prison, even for small offenses."

He went on to say, "I liked this young man, but had no recourse but to give him two years, hoping that six months would see him paroled.

"But before passing sentence, one of the strangest events in my career occurred. The young man's attorney approached me and said, 'I have something I want to share with you before you sentence my client.' He opened his briefcase and handed me a letter he had just received from the boy's father. I still have it.'"

He went to a filing cabinet, extracted a letter, and handed it to me, saying, "Here. You read it."

In the letter, the boy's father made no attempt to defend his son's behavior. Instead, he assumed full responsibility for it. Here, in part, is what he wrote:

"If Jim has to serve time in prison, try to get the judge to send me instead. After all, if I had been a better father, Jim wouldn't have gotten into this trouble. Therefore, I deserve the punishment, not him."

"How did you handle the sentencing?" I asked. "Even though the father offered to go to jail for his son, I know that one person cannot serve time for another."

The judge replied, "I gave the young man six months' probation.

"But," he continued, "I got an enormous amount of flack from the prosecuting attorney's office. My reasoning, however, was that if a parent of a sixteen-year-old could accept the full responsibility, the boy was going to get the kind of attention he needed from then on."

"I'm curious," I said. "Have you had any follow-up on how the young man turned out?"

"As a matter of fact, I have," the judge replied. "Just last summer, I bumped into his attorney, and he told me the young man had gone on to college, done very well, and was now a successful real-estate broker.

"I thank the Lord for two things in this case," the judge observed.

"What are they?" I asked.

"First, I bet on the father's good sense of responsibility, and a productive life was salvaged because of it. The father was bright enough to see where the responsibility really lay. And second, I don't have on my conscience a needlessly wasted life. I'm thankful I didn't let myself be swayed by the negativity of the prosecutor, who wanted to see that boy put in with a bunch of hardened criminals."

## Six Good Examples That Get Positive Results

Commit the following to memory: The examples we set determine the performance of the people we wish to motivate. Set good examples and you'll get good performances; set bad examples and you'll get bad performances. Below are six examples that will get excellent results in motivating others to help you win.

### Six Excellent Examples the Potter (You) Can Set

*1. Support and speak positively of higher-level people and the company you work for.* Do this and you'll inspire the people who report to you.

*2. Do your personal business on your own time.* Break this rule and soon others will be breaking it, too.

*3. Speak optimistically about everything all the time.* The best way to beat pessimism is to stop thinking and talking about how bad everything is.

*4. Take sick leave only when you're really sick.* A fact of life is, the more sick time the manager takes, the more sick time support personnel take.

*5. Build up your support personnel in front of others.* Do this and you build their morale.

*6. Treat customers as though they were special guests in your home.* Your support people will do the same. Result: more business.

## Your Job Is Getting Others to Perform Well

A motivation seminar I presented last November was attended by people from nearly every walk of life. During the seminar, we had an in-depth discussion of the concept, "You are judged not by what you do, but rather by what you cause other people to do."

When the discussion was finished, I asked everyone to write a brief description of what the concepts meant in their lives. Here are a few examples of their responses:

A salesman said, "My success is determined by my ability to cause people to buy from me, become repeat customers, and recommend both me and my products to others."

A minister said, "What I achieve in my calling is measured by my ability to bring people into my congregation, to attract new people to our group, encourage them to lead better lives, and to encourage spiritual and financial support for both the church and its activities."

A teacher said, "In the final analysis, I'm measured by the things I help my students to learn, by their conduct, the habits they develop, and how well they ultimately serve society."

A physician said, "Part of my mission is to treat sick people. But in a larger sense, my purpose is to encourage people to take care of themselves, adopt good health habits, and break bad ones."

A manager said, "I'm evaluated by my ability to get other people to meet their quotas, avoid accidents, reduce employee turnover, build enthusiasm, and speak well of our company to others."

A parent said, "I'm being tested by my ability to love my spouse, rear our children to become well adjusted and productive adults, help provide financial security, stand by when the going gets tough, and create a happy home."

Notice that people came to realize that their mission in life is getting other people to do something: work, buy, sacrifice, recommend, cooperate, invest, win, achieve. In other words, getting others to perform some kind of positive action.

Success-oriented people who want to win big see themselves as catalysts, as human agents that can make good things happen.

## Apply These Seven Magic Leadership Rules to Win More

Leadership, like all basic success tools, is simple when we apply seven easy-to-follow rules.

*1. Take good care of your personnel.* The people working for Manager A are motivated when they get more advantages than Manager B gets for his staff.

An army combat veteran explained it to me this way: "Our unit had a terrific captain. If one of the guys got into trouble, he'd help solve the problem. He always made sure we had plenty of food, the best available shelter, and the supplies we needed. In combat situations, the captain had no trouble getting us to do what we had to do. That was one way of repaying him for taking care of our basic needs."

In business, athletics, government, or any kind of organization, personnel support the manager who gives first priority to their needs. Smart managers know their support people hold the key to their success. When a manager goes out of his or her way to help an employee, great results will follow.

*2. Build pride in support personnel.* Have you ever met a good employee who told you he worked for a bad organization? Of course not. There is a direct relationship between the pride an individual takes in the company and his or her job performance.

No pride leads to bad performance. Lots of pride leads to terrific performance. An executive of a very successful convenience store chain told me he spends more time on building pride in his company than on anything else.

"As you know," he explained, "turnover, absentee-ism, and pilferage are only a few of the problems we have in the business. But I minimize those problems by paying attention to the pride factor. I hold frequent area meetings for store managers, and we seem to be in agreement that we're the best in the business.

"I supply sharp uniforms," he added. "I have a pay-for-performance compensation program. In everything I do, I consider the pride factor. People will always 'play' better for a winner than they will for a loser."

"Your emphasis on pride obviously pays off," I commented. "I understand your profits tripled in only three years."

"Pride does pay," the executive said. "Because my managers take pride in serving people, and in keeping the stores clean and properly stocked, we attract a lot more business."

Take more pride in the organization you serve and you'll enjoy more job success. And if, for some reason, you simply can't take pride in the organization you serve, look for a job with a company you can feel good about.

*3. Show courage.* We don't build statues, pay high salaries, award plaques, or show appreciation to cowards. That's a fact of life.

Instead, we admire people who have the courage to do the difficult, the stamina to keep on trying when the odds are against them. All great ventures are headed by people who have the resolve to go against the odds and give their cause everything they have. Some of our nation's earliest leaders were people of outstanding courage, and they paid an enormous price. Consider these facts about the signers of our Declaration of Independence.

Five signers were captured by the British as traitors. At least a dozen of the fifty-six had their homes ransacked and burned. Two lost their sons in the Continental Army. Another had two sons captured. Several took part in various battles of the American Revolution, and many suffered wounds or other physical hardships.

What kind of men were they? Twenty-five were lawyers or jurists. Eleven were merchants. Nine were farmers or large plantation owners. They were men of means and education. Yet they signed the Declaration of Independence, knowing full well that if they were captured, the penalty could be death.

When these courageous men signed the Declaration, they pledged their lives, their fortunes, and their sacred honor to the cause of freedom and independence.

Richard Stockton returned to New Jersey in the fall of 1776 to find the state overrun by the enemy. He removed his wife to safety, but was himself captured. His home, his fine library, his writings—all were destroyed. Stockton was so badly treated in prison that his health was ruined, and he died before the war's end.

Carter Braxton was a wealthy planter and trader. One by one, his ships were captured by the British Navy. He loaned a large sum of money to the American cause; it was never paid back. He was forced to sell his plantations and mortgage his other properties to pay his debts.

Thomas McKean was so hounded by the British that he had to move his family almost constantly. He served in the Continental Congress without pay, and kept his family in hiding.

Vandals or soldiers or both looted the properties of Ellery, Clymer, Hall, Heyward, Middleton, Harrison, Hopkinson, and Livingston.

At the Battle of Yorktown, Thomas Nelson, Jr., noted that the British General Cornwallis had taken over the family home for his headquarters. Nelson urged General George Washington to open fire on his own home. This was done, and the home was destroyed. Nelson later died bankrupt.

Francis Lewis also had his home and properties destroyed. The enemy jailed his wife for two months, and that and other hardships from the war so affected her health that she died only two years later.

"Honest John" Hart was driven from his wife's bedside when she was near death. Their thirteen children fled for their lives. Hart's fields and his gristmill were laid waste. While eluding capture, he never knew where his bed would be the next night. His wife was dead and his children gone when he returned.

Such are the stories and sacrifices typical of those who risked everything to sign the Declaration of Independence. Those men were not wild-eyed, rabble-rousing ruffians. They were soft-spoken men of means and education. They had security, but they valued liberty more, were willing to commit themselves totally: "For the support of this declaration, with a firm reliance on the protection of the Divine Providence, we mutually pledge to each other, our lives, our fortunes, and our sacred honor."

These people followed the leadership rule of courage. They will always be admired.

In business, it takes courage to promote an idea for a new product or an expansion program during a recession, or a change in company policy. Even if the proposed change is not adopted, you always gain respect when you display real courage.

*4. When you're wrong, admit it.* Some people will never become leaders because they think it's a sign of weakness to admit they're wrong. But imperfection is perhaps the most human of characteristics. Actually, people admire us when we admit we're wrong.

A manager who works for the Corps of Engineers related this incident to me. He said, "The chief of our division was an absolute autocrat. His word was it. Once, when it was time to approve the final plans to construct a levee, he changed a key part of the plan. The design engineers told him that his redesign would cause a major flooding problem. 'I'm right, now do it my way!' was his response.

"Well, they did it his way, and sure enough, a flooding problem resulted. Even with that, the division chief wouldn't admit he made a mistake. He tried to blame the staff for failing to understand what he had ordered."

"What happened?" I asked.

"The Corps finally persuaded him to take early retirement. It wasn't just one mistake that caused his downfall, but a long series of mistakes. For years, his arrogant, dictatorial 'I'm in charge' attitude impressed his superiors, but his overbearing manner finally led to his downfall."

*5. Seek the advice of support personnel.* An excellent leadership concept is to listen to people who have knowledge but lack the authority to express it.

A chief executive officer for one of the nation's largest corporations chatted with me on this point recently during a visit to Hilton Head Island.

"Look," he said, "when it comes to needing advice, I've got all the sources anyone could want. We've got more than two hundred fifty MBAs working for the company—experts in everything you can think of.

"But," he went on, "my most trusted, and often the best qualified advisor I have, is my secretary. We've been together for fifteen years. When I ask her opinion on anything, like whether a certain key spot could be filled by a certain person, or should we acquire another company, or do you think the new package will sell, I get an honest, candid answer. And more often than not, her opinion proves right. She may only have the title of senior executive secretary, but I've learned it pays to sound her out."

The CEO makes an important point. Smart engineers ask mechanics for suggestions. Systems analysts seek suggestions from programmers. Smart marketing managers get opinions from salespeople.

The point is, we can acquire a lot of ideas by going down the organization ladder for advice. Brains are distributed throughout the organization, not just located inside the management offices.

6. *Always act, think, and talk like a professional.* Based upon my observations of many different kinds of enterprises, I would say that most of them are not run by professionals. Instead, amateurs are pretty much in control. Success-oriented people, those who want more, must know the difference.

A professional is trained to do a job and perform each task with exceptional competency. A professional gives everything he or she has to the activity at hand. An amateur gives the impression he or she is engaging in a hobby. Amateurs do their work superficially, carelessly, and incompetently.

Keep in mind, however, that many so-called professionals in medicine, law, education, and other fields that require long years of persistent training are really only amateurs. Professionalism is indicated more by attitude than by diplomas and certificates.

Organizations that are unusually successful are run by true professionals. I talked with the head of an important engineering firm recently about professionalism in his particular field. His comment to me was, "We absolutely insist on professionalism in everything we do. I expect our personnel to act, talk, and think like professionals, and that means everybody—the young people who deliver blueprints, the receptionists, the secretaries, and everybody else. Nothing destroys credibility faster in our field than people who behave like amateurs."

Ask yourself, would you want anything less than a completely professional physician attending you? Or an amateur lawyer handling one of your legal problems? Smart people depend on professionals, whether it be for lawn care or preparing a tax return.

The point is, if you want to be a leader, you must think like a professional.

*7. Set the example you want others to follow.* Setting the right example is the most critical rule of all for becoming an effective leader. I became good friends with an office manager who had been with the same company for thirty years before retiring. We had an interesting conversation in Florida a few months ago.

He told me that in all the years he had been with the company, he had seen a lot of managers come and go.

"The interesting thing," he commented, "was how quickly the support people adapted their behavior to what they thought the new manager wanted. Support personnel, a little like children, quickly note what pleases or displeases the boss, and then perform accordingly."

"Please explain," I asked.

"Sure. It's like this. If a manager started coming to work late, very soon his key people began doing the same thing. If the manager cussed a lot, soon the staff began using foul language, too. If he showed disrespect for customers, it wasn't long before they were doing the same thing."

He continued, "If I learned anything during my long stay with the company, it was this: People are going to do as the boss does, and not as he says."

The question asked most by people in training to be

effective leaders is, "Am I setting the example I want others to follow? Is my conduct worthy of imitation?"

Review these principles often to help you win more.

- Your success is determined by what you cause other people to do.
- Learn the lesson Moses learned—delegate, delegate, and delegate some more.
- Remember, you are the potter, your support personnel are the clay.
- Practice the we-will-win philosophy. It brings victory in all the games we play.
- Make sure you set the example you want followed. We train others more by example than in any other way.
- Apply these rules and become a more effective leader:
    a) Take good care of your personnel.
    b) Build pride in other people.
    c) Show courage all the time.
    d) When you're wrong, admit it.
    e) Seek the advice of your support personnel.
    f) Act, think, and talk like a professional.
    g) Set the example you want followed.

# 4

# Feed Your Mind Success-Producing Information and Prosper

Your mind is extraordinarily complex. Yet it works in a simple, three-step way. First, it takes in information (what you see, hear, smell, taste, and feel). Next, it processes this information (how does what I sense relate to me?). Third, after processing the information, your brain tells you what action to take to handle it.

For example, your mind tells you it is raining (information input). You don't want to get wet (information process). So you put on a raincoat (action on the processed information).

In building a life of success or failure, your mind takes in information, processes it, and then consciously and subconsciously tells you what to do. Notice that whatever you do or say begins with information input or what you allow to get into your mind.

A cliché of modern times often heard around people who work with computers (and the human mind is the prototype for those machines) is "garbage in, garbage out." Put in incorrect or bad data and the processed information will be misleading. Finally, the action taken on the processed data will be incorrect, or "garbage."

Looked at positively, if we put in correct data, we can

expect to get accurate results. A key step in achieving more is to make sure the right kind of information is put into your mind for processing, which in turn leads to the right kind of action.

## Protect Your Mind: It's a Multimillion-Dollar Asset

Assume you own and have in your physical possession a million dollars in gold. Would you protect it? Of course, and with care. You might have electronic devices installed, hire guards, insure its safety, or take whatever action you feel is needed.

Now your mind is worth far more than a million dollars. Your mind is the exclusive source of all you will create spiritually and materialistically in your life. Your level of happiness, security, contributions to others, your dreams, all come from one place—your mind.

But do we protect our minds as carefully as we protect our physical assets (which, of course, come from the mind in the first place)? The answer is no. We allow all kinds of psychological junk information to penetrate our thought processes.

Typically, people allow gossip, rumors, news of scandals, murders, embezzlements, bankruptcies, bribery, and other miscellaneous negative information to enter their mental computer. And as a result, too many people feel, act, and even look miserable. They are, in fact, failures by any standard we choose to use.

The "bad, terrible world is coming to an end" mind-polluters come from two sources: (1) People we associate with on a day-to-day basis—the personal snipers—and (2) the media—the mass snipers. Both can limit, even destroy, your chances for your goal of more.

## Guard Against One-on-One Snipers— They're Devils with Bad News

Most departments within organizations have a sniper—a chronic bearer of bad news, a person who takes joy in interpreting current company events as being ominous. A sniper enjoys filling you in about the mistakes the department head is making; how you are likely to be hurt by some new policy; how unfair it was to promote Liz; how badly you and your associates are underpaid and mistreated, and how great it would be to get another, better-paying job.

Snipers usually are part of government or private bureaucracies and therefore have considerable job security. Usually also, they are not stupid, but intelligent and perceptive. There is always enough credibility in what the sniper says to scare people who don't recognize them for what they are—devils who create and spread bad news.

Chances are you know a sniper and are to some degree under his or her influence. So what can you do about it? Here are four suggestions:

1. Politely, let the sniper know you are too busy to talk. A person I know who works for the Corps of Engineers told me his secret. "Every week, Bud (the department sniper) would visit me three or four times to fill me in on assorted goof-ups, administrative problems that were going unsolved, and impending changes that would be disastrous. Since Bud outranked me and was older, I'd listen. Often his gossiping would go on for thirty minutes or longer. Finally, every time Bud would come into my office, I'd explain, 'I'm way behind on this project,' or 'I'm swamped right now,' and say I was too busy to talk. After about a month, Bud dropped me from his information visitation schedule and I no longer have to put up with his analysis of what is wrong."

2. Another technique that works with a sniper is *don't agree or disagree with anything he or she says.* Just sit there, ask no questions, make no comments, and sooner or later the sniper will scratch you from his or her list of people to try to frighten today. A person I know who uses this approach told me, "It's amazing how soon people will stop bothering you with bad news if they discover it doesn't worry you." The favorite targets of snipers are people with a natural inclination to worry, express concern with the issue presented, or who are relatively new to the organization.

3. Third, and this is the most direct method for dealing with snipers, is to *tell the person politely but firmly that you prefer to rely on official information, not on his or her opinions or interpretations of rumors that float around.* A woman who works as an administrator of a hospital told me, "I didn't like to do it, but I finally said to Martha, 'Look, I've got enough difficulties dealing with dozens of problems. When changes are going to be made around here, I'll learn about them.' Martha hasn't bothered me since with a new crisis that will break anytime."

4. *Suggest to the sniper that he or she find another job if this place is so bad.* One fellow I know in a large accounting firm used this tactic on a chronic sniper. "It took three encounters with that character [the sniper], but he finally knew how I felt about his petty, 'bite the hand that feeds you' method. And he no longer bothers me." Remember, such organizational snipers for some evil reason want you to worry, distrust your immediate leader and the organization as a whole, and join them in an underhanded movement against progress. Birds of a feather *do* flock together. Make sure you aren't tricked or coerced into joining the birds that are flying in circles and, perhaps, are already headed for crash landings.

## Enjoy Adventure or "Stay Close to Shore"

When I was a student, an instructor in corporation finance invited the head of a small bank to be a guest speaker. The lecture was lousy and I remember none of it. But I do remember clearly the summary statement the banker made to the class. "Young people," he said, "let me give you some advice I hope you'll put to use in your business careers. It is this: 'Stay close to shore.'"

What the banker said translates into "don't take risks," "you're secure when you play it safe," "avoid trying anything new—you might fail," and "better play the game of life close to the chest."

"Stay close to shore!" Can you think of any worse advice for young people? Suppose Henry Ford had reasoned, "I'll play it safe and build a few cars for the Detroit market. Making cars for the masses all over the nation is foolish. There are almost no paved roads, hardly any gas stations, and I have only a handful of dealers to sell cars."

It's the individuals who dare to venture far from shore who enjoy the most satisfaction, make the most money, and do the most good for other people. When only a teenager, Dr. Von Braun set his sights on the moon, and eventually he helped men land there. Jimmy Carter and Ronald Reagan, both born in America's hinterlands, left the shore and became presidents. Eighty percent of today's millionaires came from families of poor or only modest means.

Had Columbus decided to "stay close to shore," America might have remained undiscovered for another century. The stay-close-to-shore approach will never produce a millionaire, a successful business, or a truly satisfied person.

Now, unfortunately, most people you know socially or at work buy the stay-close-to-shore philosophy. They live their lives in quiet terror. And they feel more comfortable with their own sorry existence if they can sell their "don't rock the boat" approach to you. Most people close to you will tell you, "There's risk in that investment—I wouldn't touch it," or "if you move from St. Louis to Jacksonville, think of all the headaches—making new friends, getting used to a different climate, finding another house and a school for the kids. Besides, your new job is not guaranteed," or "You've got twelve years in the pension plan. If you change companies, you won't get all your contributions back."

Instead of listening to those miserable folks who want company, try your ideas on people who are making things happen—the modern-day explorers who have kept their childlike enthusiasm alive. Those people—and they are a small minority—who have elected to leave the shore of guarantees, certainties, no risks, and less is better, and are winning the game of life will help you in any way they can.

Look at it this way: Losers want—yes, they *want*—to see you lose, too. And winners want you to win.

## Will Put Himself to the Test and Made It

About two years ago, a former student, Will B., arranged to see me. "I have a big decision to make," Will began, "and I'd like to have your input."

I assured Will I'd be glad to give an opinion and asked him to explain.

"Well," Will began, "for two years I've had a fairly decent job in the customer-service department of a large office-products company. A couple of weeks ago, the sales manager of one of the divisions offered me a job in sales. My problem is, I don't know whether to accept it."

I told Will he should feel proud, because the company he works for is exceptionally selective in choosing its salespeople.

"I am flattered to be asked," Will went on, "but there are complications."

"Such as?" I asked.

"For one thing," Will continued, "only about one in three people who go into sales for the company makes it. The others fail."

I tried to assure Will that he could make it if he put forth his best efforts.

"But I've got other concerns," Will hastened to explain. "You see, my girlfriend and I plan to marry in three months. She has a job as a secretary. But the sales job is straight commission. If I don't succeed, we'll have to postpone the wedding—maybe for a long time—because there's no way we can live on her income alone."

"Is that your only misgiving?" I asked.

"No," Will replied. "The other people in the service department think I would be making a big mistake if I went into sales. Our jobs in customer service are pretty safe. During the last recession, none of us got laid off, but some of the salespeople really had it rough when our customers cut back on spending.

"And on top of that," Will continued, "my dad thinks giving up my job in customer service would be a bad mistake. He says the only way I should even consider going into sales is if the company guarantees me my old job back if I don't make it."

Almost without thinking, I said, "Good."

"What do you mean, 'good'?" Will asked. "It seems

to me it's only fair to me if I don't succeed in selling for them to give me my old job back.'"

"On the surface, it seems that way," I replied, "but your company doesn't want to give you an escape hatch. They know from lots of experience that if an employee thinks, 'I can always get my safe, same job back,' that person will not put forth his best effort. You wouldn't marry your girlfriend if you knew she'd leave you the first time you had an argument, would you?"

"Of course not," Will responded, "but all things considered, I guess I'd better keep my present job. As the old saying goes, 'A bird in the hand is worth two in the bush.'"

"Sounds to me as though you've made up your mind," I commented. "If so, you're wasting your time and mine. But let me suggest this: Before you make your decision, talk to at least two of the most successful salespeople in the company and get their advice. Based on what you've told me, and with due respect for your girlfriend, your dad, and your co-workers, so far you've discussed this only with people who aren't equipped to give you fair and impartial advice."

A year passed and I got a call from Will. "Remember that discussion we had about my going into sales?" Will began. "Well, I did what you recommended; I talked with some of the real sales pros in the company. They opened my eyes. They convinced me if I ever wanted to rise above the mediocre, I'd have to put myself to the test."

"How are you doing?" I asked. "You sound great!"

"I feel great, but I need some more advice," Will replied with laughter in his voice.

I answered, "Now what?", pretending to be irritated.

"Just this," Will said with old-fashioned enthusiasm. "Can you recommend a good investment? I'm making more money than I ever believed possible."

Will's experience has a twofold message:

1. Get advice from people who see the real picture, not those who project their own fears onto what you are considering doing.

2. Enjoy the excitement of putting yourself to a real test. Discover who you really are! Focus on the big!

## What to Say About Your Previous Employer

In my work, I've gotten to know executive-search specialists. Often called headhunters, these people specialize in matching people with key job openings. And the executive-search specialists better be right most of the time or they lose the confidence—and commissions—of the client who retains them. One search specialist, Helena B., explained it to me this way: "I earn a very good income because my recommendations work out for the client company about eighty-five percent of the time. That's over a three-year period. You see, if I recommend someone to a client and the person fails, much of my credibility for future recommendations is lost."

I told Helena I could understand that her reputation was on the line with every recommendation. But I was curious about why she was so successful in matching people and jobs.

"We use all sorts of techniques to evaluate people before we recommend them to a client," Helena explained. "We give them a battery of psychological tests, check references discreetly, run credit reports. We're very good at what we do."

"But, Helena," I said, "you've seen a lot of your colleagues come and go because they've been wrong in their recommendations. You must be doing something different or certainly better than they. What is it?"

Laughing a little, Helena said, "Some of them, I guess, were in too much of a hurry to earn their commission. But seriously, I have a technique that works wonders for me. I always probe in depth the applicant's attitude toward the job he or she now has or recently had. I ask a number of questions, some of them purposely leading, such as 'What didn't (or don't) you like about Company A? or 'What is your overall impression of the company?' 'Why did you leave?' 'Would you recommend your former employer to someone else?' When I'm seriously considering recommending a person to a client company, I spend a lot of time on this line of questioning."

"Just what are you looking for?" I asked. "Anyone looking for another job must find something in their present job they don't like."

"Well," Helena continued, "if an applicant is negative about his or her most recent employment relationship, I must assume he or she will be negative about the next employer as well. After all, most of our applicants were most recently employed in big companies. Now a big company can't be all bad or it would not have gotten to be big.

"On the other hand," Helena explained, "if the applicant has positive comments about the present or past employer, I'm much more likely to recommend him or her to the client. Comments like, 'The A Company is a fine organization, but I'm looking for even more opportunity,' or 'My immediate superior is only three years older than I, so I see my chances for advancement aren't good' set well with me.

"Let me cite a specific example," Helena went on,

now really warming up to her favorite topic—her job. "Last month, I interviewed two men for the same job. Both of them worked for the same company and in the same department! Apparently, neither of them knew the other was looking for a job. Both checked out fine on the tests. Their references were okay and the employment checks were good. The one essential difference was their attitude toward the company they both worked for.

"Bill was very positive. He explained he liked his present employer but he wanted another job to 'make more money and move up faster,' both good reasons, I thought. But Jim couldn't stop telling me about how bad his present employer was. He brought up all sorts of negatives, like favoritism in promotion, having to work about one weekend in four, even how bad the food was in the cafeteria—especially on Fridays! It goes without saying that I recommended Bill."

The point: When someone asks you about your present or past employer, say good things and then shut up! Finding fault with your present or past employers makes you—not them—look bad.

When you're being interviewed for a job, never badmouth your previous employer. And when you're talking with a prospective employee, always listen to what he or she has to say about his or her previous or current employer. If you have any doubt about this advice, think about it in somewhat more personal terms.

During a lifetime, most people have several serious romances. Young people fall in and out of love many times before a relationship becomes serious enough to result in marriage.

And as we all know, a lot of marriages don't work. Now marriage is a complicated relationship and the causes for failures are many. Strangely, many peple fail at marriage more than once!

Certainly a lot of first-time failures and most second-time marital throw-in-the-towel situations could be averted if a discerning party understood the preventive medicine contained in this conversation:

Beth and Bob, both of whom had previously been in love with other partners, are discussing their future.

Beth: "Bob, tell me, what was your relationship with Betty (Bob's former girlfriend) really like?"

Bob: "Well, to be honest and straight to the point, I couldn't stand her."

Beth: "Why? She looks and acts fine to me."

Bob: "She may look okay, I guess. But she is the most domineering person I ever met. Everything goes her way or it doesn't go."

Beth: "There are a lot of strong-willed women. Is that the only reason you no longer love her?"

Bob: "Her 'do it my way or else' is enough reason. But on top of that, you just wouldn't believe how selfish she is. It was never, 'Where would you like to have dinner tonight?' It was always, 'I've decided it would be nice to eat at such and such a place.'"

Beth: "All of us have favorite restaurants, Bob. Are you sure you're not exaggerating her self-interest?"

Bob: "Maybe I could stand her domineering attitude and her selfishness, but there's a lot more. Her friends were a bunch of idiots; I didn't like her family; I can't stand playing tennis. And I didn't like the way she treated me in front of other people."

Beth: "So you'd rate her pretty much a zero?"

Bob: "No, less than a zero. I hope I never see her again."

Now, after the above conversation, assume you are Beth. Would you have any more serious thoughts about a permanent relationship with Bob? Chances are, you would not. The longer Bob expounded on what was wrong with Betty, the more you (Beth) came to her defense. You would reason, "No one is all bad. The problem likely is with Bob."

Suppose, on the other hand, Bob had simply said, "Betty is a fine person, but we decided we weren't quite right for each other. Now what would you like to do this evening?" Chances are, Beth would have both more respect for and interest in Bob.

The message: If you can't say something good about a past relationship, say nothing.

## Project Good News and Profit!

Part of the communication process is taking in information—what you hear, see, read, and experience. The other part of communication is putting out information—what you write, show, and explain. Now here is an absolute rule for handling information you pass along to others: Emphasize the positive and ignore the negative. In other words, if you can't say something good about another person or place or an experience, shut up! Take three or four minutes to study these examples.

## When You Speak—Even Small Talk—Speak Good News, Never Bad

Probably everyone would like to be a better conversationalist. But so often people go about it in the wrong way. Let me illustrate.

I speak before many conventions. Before I talk, I want to get a good feel of the audience. So, during a social function preceding my presentation, I try to keep my ears open and my mouth shut. Almost always I find most of the chitchat overheard is negative. Here are some samples of small talk I overheard before I spoke at a recent convention in Dallas.

One fellow is expounding about Detroit. "Worst city I've ever lived in. No spring. Just winter, summer, and half a fall! Couldn't stand the place."

Another is discussing the economy. "It's never been this bad before. I voted for the man, but if he doesn't get things shaped up soon, he won't get my vote again."

Then I overheard a woman talking about the city tour. "I didn't see anything I liked. And that place we had lunch yesterday was just terrible."

Next I tuned in to a man with football on his mind. "That new coach has got to go. If I managed my business the way he runs that team, I'd have been broke years ago."

There is a place for small talk. It serves a purpose in a world where people are often strangers. But small talk need not be negative talk. Bad-mouthing cities, colleges, coaches, Presidents, scenic tours, and a dozen other things may seem clever. But it is not. It's negative, dull, destructive, and in poor taste. And small talk nearly always takes a highly opinionated, pronounced form. Rarely is it in the form of questions (like all good conversation), such as, "What is your opinion about . . . ?" "What do you think is a good solution to . . . ?" "What do you like best about . . . ?"

## Avoid the Negative Media and Feel Better Fast

Our attitudes toward people, society, and the economy are shaped more by TV, radio, and the print media than we think. And at least 80 percent of this influence is negative—it's thought poison. Let me explain.

I attended an interesting—and exciting—"Enjoy Your Rewards and Learn Even More" meeting last January in the Caribbean. The meeting was sponsored by an insurance company as a reward for its exceptional performers. It was also an opportunity to share knowledge and techniques on how to achieve even bigger goals in the future. My assignment was to present ideas on "How to Select a Nourishing Mental Diet." My presentation dealt with how to select positive associates and friends who would lend encouragement, reinforce personal goals, and simply make one enjoy being alive even more.

After the presentation, three of the attendees and I had our own unscheduled conference. All three were in their sixties and had joined the insurance company after successful careers in other fields. One had been a minister, another was a retired police captain, and the third was a former real-estate broker. The one thing the three people had in common was extraordinary achievement with the company.

Our discussion soon got down to the topic of the afternoon—how to improve one's mental diet. (I've observed that highly motivated, successful achievers don't want to talk very long about politics, golf, football, and fishing. They love their work. Next to their families, it's the most important part of their lives. So their conversations soon focus on how they can do even better.)

Jim, the former police captain, opened up by saying he thought the afternoon's discussion on friend selection and personal pollution control was excellent, but left out a critically important part of what influences our minds and our behavior.

"What was that?" I asked.

Jim quickly responded with, "The negative impact of the media. In my law-enforcement career, I was involved in trying to solve just about every kind of crime—murder, rape, robbery, arson—you name it. But in my experience, the outrageous coverage of crime by the newspapers and radio and television simply increased the number and variety of crimes. The net effect of press coverage of crime is to increase it. For example," Jim explained, "the more bank robberies are reported, the more people try to rob banks. Same goes for murders and rapes."

"I've heard the same observation made about suicides," I commented. "The manager of a leading hotel that has a twenty-story open lobby told me that they've had nineteen suicides over the last dozen years or so. And every time someone commits suicide by jumping off a balcony, the incident gets front-page coverage in the newspapers. Thanks to the publicity, there are usually several suicide attempts over the next few days. Press coverage of suicides simply encourages other despondent people to try it."

The minister, Bill H., then noted, "I saw the same phenomenon in my church. I was a pastor of one church for sixteen years, and I saw domestic and drug problems escalate as news coverage about them increased. The more that prominent and famous people divorced, the more divorces I found in my congregation. Same is true for drugs. Somehow, the more news people hear about drug use, the more people use drugs. Domestic and drug difficulties are like a contagious disease. The more people hear about them, the more problems result."

Patricia P., the real-estate broker, said, "Well, crime and domestic problems are beyond my expertise. But in real estate, as in all businesses, we have our ups and downs. And every time the economy goes into a down cycle, the press blows it way out of proportion. Headlines like 'New Housing Starts Off Thirty Percent' or 'Inventory of Unsold Houses at All-time High' simply scare people. And the whole economy suffers.

"But," Patricia went on, "these same papers that make panic their business never refuse our ads. I think newspapers do more to hold down economic growth than anything in our society."

As we continued our discussion, Jim W., the police chief, said to me, "I think we've agreed that bad news simply creates more bad news. But what can we do about it? Bad news hurts everyone, except perhaps the media. They make money telling bad news. Is there some way to avoid the mind-crippling impact of the media?"

## How to Deal with the Negative Media

I've given that conversation a lot of thought. Here are some specific suggestions to deal with media-directed mental pollution:

*1. Recognize that much of what you hear and read is simply untrue.* One example of thousands of media lies told every year was a series of articles by a reporter for one of the nation's most prominent newspapers. The articles dealt with the life of a heroin addict. The reporter did such a great job describing the horror of this addict that she won a Pulitzer Prize, the highest possible journalism award. Later, it was discovered that the reporter had invented the whole story. The reporter was writing pure fiction, no facts at all!

It is impossible to describe how badly the news is distorted. Look at it through your perspective. Chances are you want a nice, spacious place to live, good food, fine automobiles, advantages for your children, vacations, heat in the winter and air conditioning in the summer. You want the good life.

But the media tell you (a) you can't have these things because we're running out of resources and (b) if you are patriotic, you'll enjoy doing with less. Headlines scream at you, saying:

"Mass Starvation Inevitable"

"Energy Crisis to Grow Worse"

"Pollution Will Kill All People in Twenty Years"

"Standard of Living Will Plunge"

"Population Is Out of Control"

Now these headlines and their supporting evidence are simply not true. They are lies intended to sell newspapers, magazines, and books. People who write and talk about the impending disasters don't bother with the truth. They prefer to manufacture sensation instead.

Julian L. Simon, an economist, studied the facts about the awful conditions the world faces. His study was careful and comprehensive. He wrote about his findings in a book, *The Ultimate Resource,* published by Princeton University Press. Chances are this book will never become popular, but it should. It is by far the most definitive analysis of our economic future written in this century—possibly ever. Just a few of Dr. Simon's conclusions are:

- "The potential reserves for all the important minerals are sufficient for many lifetimes, on the basis of almost any assumption about whether resources are 'really' finite or not."[1]
- "There is no necessity either in logic or in histor-

[1] Julian Simon, *The Ultimate Resource* (Princeton, N.J.: Princeton University Press, 1981), p. 40.

ical trends to suggest that the supply of any given resource is 'finite.'"[2]

- "There is little reason to believe that, in the foreseeable long run, additional people will make food more scarce and more expensive."[3]
- "Farmers—especially in the U.S.—are pushing for subsidies to reduce the food production."[4]
- "There is no basis for opposition to continuing economic and population growth."[5]
- "If one has to choose a single measure of the state of pollution, the most plausible one . . . is life expectancy. And the expected length of a newborn's life has increased greatly in past centuries and is still increasing."[6]
- "The notion of 'untrammeled' copulation represents either ignorance or arrogant untruth."[7]
- "A larger population implies a larger amount of knowledge being wasted. . . . This is the straightforward result of there being more people to have new ideas."[8]
- "Is the stock of agricultural land being depleted? Just the opposite. The world's total stock of agricultural land is increasing."[9]
- "The main fuel to speed our progress is our stock of knowledge, and the brake is our lack of imagination. The ultimate resource is people—skilled, spirited, and hopeful people. . . ."[10]

Take your choice. Believe what a true objective expert has learned. Or, if you prefer, believe the doom-and-gloom headlines people in search of fame and promotion like to invent.

[2]Ibid., p. 50.  [5]Ibid., p. 89.  [8]Ibid., p. 210.
[3]Ibid., p. 61.  [6]Ibid., p. 143.  [9]Ibid., p. 239.
[4]Ibid., p. 80.  [7]Ibid., p. 187.  [10]Ibid., p. 348.

If you really want more, believe the conclusion that there is plenty. If you want less, believe the unfounded, stupid prophecies of doom.

*2. Understand that bad news makes more bad news, and good news makes more good news.* Learn this law and apply it and watch good things happen. When we stop preaching bad news and start promoting good news, we attract more friends, win greater support, enjoy life a lot more and make more money. Let's see why.

A young manufacturer's agent I know, Fred K., deals in used, inexpensive furniture. His operation is simple— and profitable. He buys used furniture from motels and hotels and then resells it to used-furniture stores. While sharing ideas one day at lunch, Fred explained a discovery he had made that reflects directly on the bad = bad, good = good law.

"I have two salesmen who sell the furniture I buy to furniture stores. Last year, Salesman A sold three times as much furniture as Salesman B. I was determined to find out why, because their territories were very similar and I knew I would make a lot more profit if Salesman B sold as much as Salesman A.

"What I did," Fred continued, "was select six retailers in A's territory and six in B's territory. I talked to these retailers and I soon found the difference. In a nutshell, when retailers asked Salesman A questions such as 'How's the product moving?,' he'd tell them, 'Great. All you have to do is promote it the right way.' (Then he'd show them how to resell the merchandise.) When B was asked a similar question, he'd reply, 'Well, things are slow right now, but with a little luck, conditions will improve.'

"Or when a retailer asked Salesman A, 'How is your price increase going to affect our sales?,' he'd reply with something like, 'It means you'll make more money per unit sold. And customers probably won't even notice the increase. If they object, remind them that the furniture is a bargain. The motels that supply us obviously sell their furniture while it's still in good condition.' The result: Most retailers would buy in good quantities.

"But," Fred went on, "when a retailer complained about a price increase to Salesman B, he would go off on some tangent about how bad inflation is, how tough it is to make money these days, and how unemployment is headed up. Or when a retailer asked Salesman B how the product was moving, he'd tell them it varied. And that they would have to spend a lot on advertising if they wanted it to sell."

Then Fred told me, "I had to let B go. I hated to, because despite his negativism, he needed the job. But his spreading bad news was cutting profits way back."

The point: Supply good news with the merchandise and make more money; give bad news with the product and make less—or lose—money.

Now the law that bad news makes more bad news and good news makes more good news applies in everything we do individually or as a society. Note these observations:

A "respected" stock-market advisor told subscribers to his newsletter that stock prices would crash on a certain Monday. Like sheep, they believed his bad news, and sure enough, stock prices collapsed on that Monday.

News about bank robberies, murders, and rapes causes more robberies, murders, and rapes.

News about arson always sets off a rash of more intentionally set fires.

Information about the achievements of young people results in more young people putting forth their best efforts.

Meanwhile, news of businesses' success produces more business successes. Simply put, good news promotes business—leads to expansion, improvement, and profit. Bad news puts the brakes on business—leads to cutbacks, retrenchment, and postponement.

Bad news really does make more bad news. Terrorism is a major problem right now. It is certain to get massive coverage in the media. And that is the goal—mass-media coverage—that terrorists seek. In fact, it is common after a bomb goes off someplace for two, three, or even four different terrorist gangs to claim credit for the atrocity. They want the free publicity (advertising) that the media gives them. An experienced law-enforcement man in New York made a suggestion with which intelligent people will agree: "Let the police do their job and the press stay out of it."

The intentional starvation of prisoners in Ireland some years ago got tremendous publicity. Every major newscast for months gave prominent mention to the condition of these starving, self-proclaimed heroes. Soon other prisoners all over the world had picked up on this great plan and started starving themselves to gain concessions from prison officials. Without prominent news coverage, the starvation epidemic would never have gotten off the ground.

Hostage-taking, too, is one of the media's favorite topics. And so are airplane hijackings. So much publicity was given to hijackers when the activity was first popularized in the press that an elaborate—and enormously expensive—detection system had to be installed.

The media philosophy is bad = good; terrible = terrific; and horrible = stupendous. Make no mistake about it: The media is the dominant influence over what we think and, therefore, how we behave. And the media, whether by design or by accident, corrupts your thinking—and thereby your behavior. The media, America's cause of "Cancer of the Thinking Apparatus," believes bad news is good for their business.

Examples:

1.  Bad news is good news. Headlines: "Local Business Goes Bankrupt" or "School Lunch Program Cut Back"

2.  Terrible news is terrific news. Headlines: "Three People Injured in Wreck—Component Part of XYZ Manufacturing Believed Responsible," or "Worst Snowstorm in Decades Paralyzes Midwest"

3.  Horrible news is the stupendous news. Headlines: "Madman Rapes, Kills Woman in Park," or "Hong Kong Flu Viruses Threaten Ten Million Senior Citizens"

On the personal level, most of us—if we are alert—know that most gossip, rumors, and "the inside scoop" are at best half-truths. If we're smart, we discount the "hey, I just heard . . ." type of information.

But what about the news we watch on TV and read in the newspapers? Most people believe information from these sources as if it were the gospel truth. If you question a friend's relay of the news to you, chances are he'll say, "But I read it in the paper," or "I saw it on TV."

Look at the distortions in these sample headlines:

"Unemployment Reaches 8 Percent." The statement might be true. But an equally true statement would be "Ninety-two Percent Are Employed." But the 8 percent or whatever figure is used is likely to be a distortion, since most people in our society who are willing and able to work can find a job. Honest unemployment—people between jobs—is never more than 2 or 3 percent of the work force. The same newspaper that carries the 8 percent or 10 percent or 6 percent or whatever unemployment statistic never carries a subhead "Fifteen Pages of Job Opportunities in the Classified Section."

Before you pay any attention to the news, answer two questions: (1) Will the information increase my spiritual prosperity, and (2) Will it increase my material prosperity?

## Will the Information Increase My Spiritual Prosperity?

An elderly woman told me not long ago why she gave up listening to bad news. "It just made me feel awful," she said, "I just couldn't believe people are as bad as they say. Every week nice folks come to see me, they show me pictures of their children, keep me up-to-date on what my friends I don't see often are doing. People are generally good until I read the paper or watch TV. Then all I see is how badly people behave. So I've given up on bad news. I simply don't pay attention to it."

She paused a moment and then went on, "Now I'll be honest. I may want to hear about the bad news just as I guess a drug addict wants more drugs. But I don't need the bad news just as the unfortunate person on drugs doesn't need another dose. I find I'm happier and feel better since I don't pay attention to the evil stories the media puts out."

News items are either spiritual lifters or spiritual downers. The spiritual lifters—good news from friends and relatives, achievements of others, scientific programs, improvements in the world around us, lift the spirit and make us feel good. But news about catastrophes in countries we've never heard of, war talk we can do nothing about, are spiritual downers. They make us worry and hurt our health.

The point: Unless the news builds your spirit, ignore it. Bad news causes cancer of the conscience.

## Will the Information Increase My Material Prosperity?

A salesman told me very simply why he gave up listening to the news on his car radio. "It's all rather discouraging," he said. "Now I make four key calls a day and I spend a lot of time driving. Listening to a reporter describe a bank robbery, an auto accident, or interview a homosexual psyches me down and my sales presentations reflect it. You see," he went on, "I played football in college. Football taught me a big lesson. You've got to be psyched up for every play. Well, the game I play now is sales, and I need all the mind control I can muster. So, on my way to see a prospect, I do one of three things: I play a motivational tape on my cassette player, I listen to a good music station, or I just think through what I should cover to make the sale. And when I meet the prospect, I've always got some good, positive news for him."

The point: Pay attention only to good news. If you don't hear any, rely on some old standbys. Tell the person you call on, "You look great," or "Hey, I've got some good news for you," or "I've got the solution to the problem you gave me last week."

In quick review, just:

- Protect your mind. It's a multimillion-dollar asset.
- Guard against the devils who transmit bad news by:
    a) Letting them know you're too busy to talk.

    b) Not agreeing or disagreeing with them.

    c) Relying on official information, not gossip.

    d) Telling the bad-news carrier to find another job if he doesn't like the company.

- Enjoy adventure. Staying close to shore gets you nowhere.
- Put yourself to the test. Prove you can do it.
- When looking for another job, always say good things about your previous employer.
- Say only good things about all your previous relationships.
- Avoid the negative media and feel better.
- Remember that good news makes more good news and bad news only makes more bad news.
- Pay attention only to news that increases your spiritual prosperity and your material prosperity.

**5**

# Want More? Then Give More

Have you ever met anyone who wanted less—less wealth, poorer health, fewer friends, or reduced status? Everyone you and I know wants more satisfaction, more of the good things in life, more wealth and enjoyment. We want that great feeling of knowing, "I am moving ahead. I have more this year than last year."

Now there are two basic approaches to getting more: Act selfishly or behave generously.

To understand how these approaches work and their results, imagine two couples: Mr. and Mrs. Selfish, and Mr. and Mrs. Generous.

Mr. and Mrs. Selfish's thought patterns are dominated exclusively by themselves, their welfare, their benefits, their pleasures. "What is in it for us?" controls their every thought and act. They think: The less we give, the more we'll have for ourselves.

Mr. and Mrs. Selfish reason, "If we sell the customers a pound of meat weighing fourteen ounces instead of sixteen ounces, we've made a gain. Or, if we give less service than is expected, we'll enlarge our profits. Or, if we pay our employees no more than the absolute minimum required by law, we'll make more money and grow rich faster."

Meanwhile, Mr. and Mrs. Generous think differently.

Their concern is directed primarily at helping others benefit, grow, enjoy life, and overcome obstacles. "How can we help and satisfy others?" influences everything they do. Sure, they, too, want more. But Mr. and Mrs. Generous's actions center on the principle that the more they give of themselves to others, the more they will receive in return.

They reason, "If we give customers more than they expect to receive, the customers will become repeat customers and in time we will make more money."

They are smart. Mr. and Mrs. Generous know if they pay employees their true worth, give them help and understanding, and do all they can to help them advance, everyone enjoys more in the long run.

Just one day spent in the real world will convince you that Mr. and Mrs. Selfish dominate in numbers and influence. But they receive surprisingly little. More of the good things in life gravitate to Mr. and Mrs. Generous.

## How Giving More Made Three Entrepreneurs in Education Wealthy

Examples of giving first-class service and receiving first-class rewards can be found in all kinds of activities. Recently, I read about a business school in the Northeast that simply could not break even despite large state subsidies. Finally, the state withdrew the supporting funds and the school closed. Subsequently, it was reopened with the backing of three young entrepreneurs. In less than eighteen months, the entrepreneurs were making a profit. Asked how they did it, their spokesman said, "We analyzed the situation and reached a single conclusion: The business school failed because the students received far less education than they were paying for.

"The instructors were mostly tenured," he continued, "and put forth at best a minimal effort. They were rarely available to help students plan their academic programs, solve difficult problems, and help them find jobs. Because of low standards, low-quality instruction, and administrative apathy, high-quality students didn't apply, and the school lost its good reputation.

"What we did," the spokesman continued, "was to make a decision to go first-class, and give the students more of what they wanted and needed. We staffed the school with people who were proven experts—competent teachers. We were not concerned with how many degrees they had. We scheduled classes to fit students' work schedules and we built pride and enthusiasm into our student body. And we let prospective employers know about the changes we made. Now we're operating at a profit, have a waiting list of applicants, and we are gaining regional support for our programs.

"We found that when you put service first, when you give students more than they expect to receive, the money problem is soon solved."

This example says a lot about the superiority of private enterprise over public bureaucracy. It also reaffirms the concept, "Want to get? Then give!"

## How to Profit More by Sharing the Result

Many managers are greedy. And greedy people think the way to make more money is to exploit, take advantage of, or simply cheat their personnel. But the approach doesn't work.

Meanwhile, a few managers are generous. They believe they should reward people fairly on the basis of performance. They believe in sharing.

Which style, greed or generosity, gets the better results? Owners of businesses and managers have debated
the question a long time. But to objective observers, the
answer is clear: The more closely monetary reward is related to how well people do their jobs, the better will be
their performances. That is a basic consideration in operating a business at a profit.

In other words, giving tied to a person's output is a
strong motivation. Let me give you an example.

About twenty years ago, a friend of mine learned how
to cook chicken breasts in a way that made them taste
especially good to customers who visited his small restaurant. He was so successful that he soon opened a second
restaurant, and a third.

Now he was faced with a question. How could he expand his chicken food chain, retain close control over his
operation so his chicken always tasted just right, and
provide incentives to his store managers so they would
work as hard as he (and that was pretty hard)?

My friend came up with three money-making decisions. First, he decided he would own all his restaurants
rather than franchise them. In this way, he would main-
tain full control over the way the stores were operated.

Next, he would select his managers with extreme
care—not just for their technical competency, but for
their moral integrity as well. He wanted store managers
who were thoroughly trustworthy and would not spend a
good share of their time trying to cheat him or provide
less than the very best service to customers.

The third part of his plan was extraordinarily inge-
nious. He decided to give each store manager a small
basic salary, a living income, and one-half the profits the
store made. Because the managers had a direct share in
the profits, they had the maximum incentive to do the
job right, to motivate their employees, to make certain

the chicken was cooked just right so that the customers were pleased.

This generous way of compensating managers helped some of them earn salaries into six figures. Almost all of them earn about double what upper-middle managers in most other companies make.

My friend, a deeply religious person, is enormously pleased with the result. "My store managers like the plan because they can earn as much as they're worth. The customers (who, of course, don't know about the compensation plan) are happy because the managers see to it that the food is cooked just right and the service is tops. And I'm happy because I'm making a lot of money and enjoying life by helping other people gain more."

Here's the point: *If you want to get a lot, give a lot.*

## It Really Is Better to Give Than Receive

We've all heard that statement many times, but it's hard to believe. Let me give you an example of why it's true.

On a plane one day, my seat companion and I got to talking about problems we've had traveling in unfamiliar locations. My friend said to me, "The most interesting situation I've ever encountered happened in northern Ohio. I had rented a car three days before and hadn't bothered to check the gas gauge, since I rarely empty a tank in a rented car.

"Well," he continued, "here I was cruising down an interstate when I ran out of gas. So I proceeded to try and hitch a ride. It was after midnight and well below freezing. I must have been out there twenty minutes before an old fellow in a pickup pulled over and asked if he could help. I explained that I had run out of gas.

"He laughed and said, 'At one time or another, it happens to all my cousins. Get in. I'll carry you to a gas station.'

"Driving down the road, I said to my benefactor, 'What made you stop? Dozens of cars passed by and didn't even slow down.'

"The old fellow glanced at me and said, 'Because you're my cousin.'

"'Sir,' I said, 'you must be mistaken. Twice you've referred to me as your cousin. I'm from North Carolina, and to the best of my knowledge, I have no relatives in Ohio.'

"'You're still my cousin,' the old fellow said. 'You see, you and I are blood kin to every other person, regardless of their nationality, where they were born, their race, religion, or what have you. And I like to help my cousins when they're in need.'

"I sat there for a few moments pondering what the old guy had said. All of us human beings are in truth cousins. Rich people, poor people, successful folks, failures—we are all kin.

"Finally, we got some gas and he drove me back to my car. The trip was at least twenty miles and I had consumed close to an hour of this fellow's time. I tried to pay him for his trouble and expense, but he wouldn't accept anything.

"In parting, he said to me, 'I like to help people. You see, I'm a deacon in a country church. And I often make a slight change in the commandment, "Do unto others the way you would have them do unto you" by saying, "Give unto others the way you would have them give unto you."

"'I hope you'll remember what happened here tonight and repay the favor by helping one of our cousins.'

"And you know," my companion continued, "the

message that my cousin the deacon gave me has done a world of spiritual good for me. Since that incident, I've found myself doing a lot more simple favors for people I don't even know. And I find that helping people with no thought of getting something in return is making more good things happen to me. It's making me a real believer in the invisible hand that seems to give direction to what we do."

The point: Provide some help with no thought of return and reward will take care of itself.

## How Valerie's Mother Is Giving to Make Life Better for the Next Generation

Recently, while I was working in my office one evening, the cleaning lady came in to take out the trash that had accumulated that day.

She said to me, "You're working rather late, aren't you, Dr. Schwartz?"

I laughed, saying, "I'm not really working, because to me work isn't work. It's fun. And it's not late; it's only ten o'clock."

"Are you working on another book?" she asked.

This surprised me, for it's unusual for most cleaning ladies to know your name and to ask what you're doing.

"The reason I ask," she went on, "is because I enjoyed *The Magic of Thinking Big* so much. My daughter gave it to me to read. Maybe you remember her. Her name is Valerie S., and she was a student of yours two or three semesters ago."

"Oh, yes," I replied, "I remember Valerie very well. She did an excellent job in class, was one of the top two or three students. And as I recall, she was fifth runner-up for Miss America. Valerie is very poised, intelligent, sophisticated, and beautiful," I observed.

But my surprise that Valerie's mother was a cleaning lady showed, and her mother recognized it immediately.

Mrs. S. looked at me, smiled, and said, "You're thinking that cleaning ladies can't have brilliant, beautiful daughters."

"No, not really," I replied. "But I envisioned Valerie's mother as living in a fancy suburban home, entertaining rich friends two or three times a week."

Then Valerie's mother broke into laughter. "I do spend much of my time in a five-bedroom home in the suburbs, and I do help give elaborate dinner parties frequently. You see, Dr. Schwartz, by day and on weekends I'm a maid in one of those fashionable homes on the North Side. And by night, I work four hours helping clean up this building.

"I'm working two jobs so Valerie and her sister can go through college with their heads high. That's why I like this second job. Now I don't think anyone enjoys emptying trash cans and dusting the desks, but it gives me a chance to help my daughters. I'm giving my children what my parents couldn't give me."

After Mrs. S. left, I thought to myself: What a beautiful spirit! What a fine attitude! Nothing is more important or more satisfying than giving of oneself to help the next generation.

Mrs. S. could do what most mothers in her circumstances would have done, been content with one job and let her daughters get by the best way they could. But she chose to give her all and hopefully improve her daughters' chances for success. Isn't that admirable!

The point: Do you love your kids? Then make every sacrifice needed to help them enjoy the maximum the world has to offer.

## One Restaurant Gives and Gets, Another Goes Bankrupt. Why?

A law that can't be repealed is, "To get, you've got to give." The law applies in every profession, occupation, and business. Assuming you are engaged in legal work, the way to riches, wealth, and more respect is to put giving first, and let getting come naturally.

If you're a chiropractor, give everything you've got to your profession and your success is guaranteed. The same rule applies if you're a computer programmer, manager, athlete, or salesman. The law, "Put service first and rewards are automatic," is as true as that day always follows night. Let me give you an example.

A few months ago, I assigned a group of students a special project. I asked them to compare the strategies of two businesses in competition for the same customers and then draw conclusions about which business is more successful, and why.

One student, Charles B., decided to compare two restaurants. He had worked several months for each establishment as a busboy and wanted to explain why Restaurant A was a great success, and Restaurant B went bankrupt.

In his report, Charles explained that the food in Restaurant A was excellent and the servings extra large. The service was prompt, courteous, and efficient. The hostess, waitresses, and cashier were friendly. And everyone smiled. Patrons were treated like royalty.

The management of Restaurant B was another story. For example, they insisted on serving very small portions of food. They couldn't understand that the cost of the food was only a small part of their total costs. Even when the restaurant was virtually empty, the hostess still seated people in the worst locations, like next to the kitchen door, or beside a service area where they kept steak sauce and that sort of thing.

Restaurant B waitresses didn't last long. Waitresses in both restaurants were paid low wages and depended on tips for most of their income. Tips were small at Restaurant B because everything about the place was negative. People tip little or nothing when they are dissatisfied with a restaurant.

Meanwhile, Restaurant A had a waiting list of applicants for waitress jobs because the service and the atmosphere were excellent and the tips were large.

Now, Charles pointed out, he had to work a lot harder in Restaurant A than in Restaurant B because there were a lot more customers. But it was a lot more fun. Restaurant A was full every evening, including Monday, which is usually a slow night for most restaurants.

As a postscript, Restaurant B went into bankruptcy. The reason: revenue insufficient to meet costs. The real reason: a manager who tried to get without giving.

## What Peter W. Learned from President Kennedy That Helped Him Succeed

In only eight years, Peter W. built a chain of sixteen home-improvement centers in a large city. He sells a wide variety of home-improvement products and services to both contractors and do-it-yourselfers.

Peter is very prosperous. I had met him a couple of times casually at business functions, but I had never had an in-depth conversation with him until we happened to have lunch together at an investment seminar we both were attending.

I jokingly asked Peter why he was attending an investment seminar, since everyone knows he is wealthy. He laughed and replied, "I guess I'm here for the same reason you are—to learn how to earn even more!" (As an aside, I've observed that people who attend seminars and conferences on how to make more money are usually folks who are already well on the road to success. People who really need the information are usually too cynical to invest in useful information.)

During lunch, I asked Peter how he had managed to build a chain of highly successful home-improvement stores in an industry known for its extreme competition and high failure.

"Well," Peter replied, "it's a long and almost incredible story, but let me give it to you in a nutshell."

"Way back in high school, the civics instructor asked the students in her class to select a quotation from a President of the United States and write an essay explaining how it relates to everyday living. If applied, how it would make us more successful.

"I read some of the things our Presidents had said and finally I came across one quotation that for some reason had profound meaning for me. It was a statement made by President John Kennedy at his inauguration. Mr. Kennedy said, 'And so, my fellow Americans, ask not what your country can do for you; ask what you can do for your country.'

"Somehow," Peter continued, "I kept thinking about Kennedy's statement in every spare moment for weeks. I think I understood what Mr. Kennedy was saying about how we as individuals relate to the nation. In other words, people should stop asking the government for welfare, handouts, and subsidies. Instead, they should try to help the government by being good citizens, making their own way, and taking a stand for patriotism.

"In thinking about the Kennedy quote, I began to see

that it applied to me personally and to what I was doing. It hit me, for example, that in playing on the football team, I was more interested in getting other players on the team to help me make big plays and score touchdowns than I was in helping the team. And in my self-examination, I found I was putting my own interests ahead of the other members of my family and the classes I attended.

"The Kennedy quote totally revised my thinking about the 'how' of achievement. Early in life I had been taught, 'The Lord helps those who help themselves,' and now I had learned something more profound and even wiser. 'The Lord helps far more those who help others.' I've applied the concept, 'Give more to others and they will give more to me,' to everything I've done in business."

"How so?" I asked.

"For one thing, in my business we never give less than full value. Traditionally, we give a free tool with a major purchase. You see," he explained, "we need the customers far more than they need us. What we can do for the customers dictates every policy we have.

"I've learned to use the same philosophy in everything I do. In my family relationship, I think only of what I can do for them, not what they can do for me. I apply the same rule in my church, my trade association, all my relationships. I never act the role of boss with my store managers and their employees. I'm their coach and help them financially and spiritually every way I can."

On returning to the next session of the investment seminar, I said to Peter, "Your application of the Kennedy principle has worked wonders for you. Why don't more people use it?"

Peter replied, "I don't know. My guess is that the

great majority of people in business simply don't understand that the give-and-get philosophy is no theory—it's a very pragmatic law."

## Respect: the Most Treasured but Rarest Gift

After many years as a business consultant, I have reached this conclusion: The basic cause of aggressive union activity, personnel turnover, absenteeism, walkouts, slowdowns, and related problems is lack of respect by managers for their employees.

If you are a manager, you won't like reading that statement. It doesn't set well. But read it again, because it is true. Personnel in many companies are not treated with as much respect as raw materials, machines, and other inanimate objects. But disrespect of people need not occur. Those few managers who do give the gift of genuine respect to the ordinary workers who make up the labor force reap wonderful results in employee loyalty and productivity.

Let me tell you about a manager who does know how to get the most from his people and doesn't have the usual problems most managers face. His name is Sam J. and he is the top manager in a snack-foods company in Tennessee.

I did some work recently with his company and got to know Sam well. Most of the work the employees do is boring, routine, dull. The tasks are highly repetitive and are basically simple. At least 50 percent of the jobs can be learned in three days or less. Despite this low-level type of work, the employees have high morale. Why?

A basic reason, I feel, is that Sam gives everything

he's got to the six hundred employees. He dresses very much like the rank-and-file employee. He's in the plant at least two hours every day talking to workers, asking them about their children, making chitchat, telling them about the good job they're doing.

Sam knows most of the employees by their first names. When one of them is hospitalized, Sam makes every effort to visit him or her. When a member of the employee's family passes on, Sam is there to pay his respects. We all know that actions say more than words, and Sam's actions say loudly and clearly, "I respect you."

Another thing Sam does is publish a good weekly paper for the employees. By good, I mean the paper stresses the things employees are really interested in: who got promoted, who got married, who had a baby, or retired, or had a birthday. All kinds of stuff that big managers think people don't care about. One day I asked Sam how he learned these giving techniques that work so well in keeping his employees happy despite the fact the working conditions aren't good.

"Well," he said, "I grew up in this town. My dad worked in this company at a very low level all of his life. But he did manage to save enough money to help me get started at the state university. I studied engineering and I made a resolution that I was going to come back and get a job with this company. My goal was to turn it around. As a youngster, I had heard my dad talk about how senior management ignored the workers' problems and did not respond to their needs, the accidents that occurred, the low pay, the miserable working conditions, and the low regard senior people had for the work force.

"When I finished school, I came here, got a job in an entry-level management position, and worked my way up. Gradually, I acquired more influence and I was able to make some improvements. Five years ago, they made me the top executive, but I'm still one of the people. Sure, I make several times as much as the highest-paid person in our production department, but they accept that. They like me because I don't try to be better than they are. I really believe," he said, "all of us are created equal in the eyes of God.

"You know," Sam went on, "I feel my biggest contribution to the company is that all the workers here know my dad was one of them. I'm the same guy he was, but my engineering education didn't make me think I'm better than they are.

"I respect every one of those workers, for each of them plays a position on our team. And because I give them respect, they don't complain about working double shifts occasionally or performing unpleasant tasks.

"You know," Sam concluded, "fancy, expensive fringe-benefit packages don't build loyalty. But showing respect does show I care about each one of the employees as an individual."

## Enjoy Making Sacrifices. They Are Investments

The word sacrifice has a negative meaning to many people because they know only half the definition of the word—the part that says "giving up something desirable." What some people don't know is the second part of the definition, which is "to gain a higher objective or something even more worthwhile."

When we learn and apply the whole meaning of the word sacrifice, we discover more joy, self-worth, and acquire more money.

Let me explain.

Tim T., an administrator for an insurance company, told me how making sacrifices paid off for him. Two years ago, Tim explained, a friend asked him to become a part-time distributor of products used in the home. Tim thanked his friend but turned down the offer because it would mean making too many sacrifices in his lifestyle, such as giving up TV, relaxing, spending time with the kids—those sorts of things.

Finally, Tim explained, after three invitations to go into business, he agreed to give it a try.

"Sure, at first there were some 'sacrifices,'" Tim explained. "I gave up watching football six or eight hours every weekend, I cut way back on my golf in the summer and my bowling in the winter, I stopped watching those TV soap operas, and I eliminated my putter-around-and-accomplish-nothing activities. I converted those meaningless time-wasters into money. That was the first benefit.

"But I benefited in three even more important ways," Tim continued. "I found by sacrificing some pointless activities, I liked myself a whole lot more. For the first time in my life, I found I was in charge of my financial future. My rewards in my own business were in direct proportion to the time, effort, and skill I put into it.

"As you know," Tim went on, "few people who work for a salary are paid for what they do. They are paid an arbitrary standard some job analyst set up—not on the basis of what they contribute."

"How else did you benefit from making what some people think are sacrifices?" I asked.

"Well, a third big reward I got," Tim explained, "was the wonderful joy in helping other people climb out of their financial pit and find a greater measure of prosperity. You see, I make money two ways—a commission on what I sell and an override on what people I bring into the business sell. Indirectly, I've helped some really fine people to afford needed dental care, buy new cars, enjoy vacations, and send their kids to college."

"But the biggest benefit of all," Tim concluded, "is the positive effect operating the part-time business has on my family. You see, my wife Jenny and I have three children—a son twelve and two daughters nine and ten. And all of them are part of the business. They help fill orders, answer the phone, make deliveries, rotate the stock to keep it fresh—things like that. Philip, our son, even operates our home computer so we know exactly what products are in stock, what we need to order from the warehouse, money owed us, and money we owe others. The whole family is included, and that brings us closer together."

(Here, Tim digressed to give his views on why kids should be part of the family's economic activity. According to Tim, helping children learn how our economic system works leads to more productivity, less crime, less reliance on drugs, and far more satisfaction with life. Tim feels children suffer from "boredomitis" more than adults.)

Perhaps not all sacrifices turn out as satisfying as those made by Tim. But as you look at sacrifice in terms of cost/benefit, remember what A. P. Goutley wrote, "To get profit without risk, experience without danger, and reward without work, is as impossible as it is to live without being born."

## Help Others Understand the Give-to-Get Philosophy

Let's be sure we have the give-to-get philosophy in proper perspective. Giving should be a reward of some kind, not a handout for doing nothing. Economists ramble on and on discussing what ails the economy—why it is difficult to balance the budget, and give people the economic freedom they need so they can experience a truly golden age.

For decades now, millions of people have been taught that it is their right to receive free goods and services from the government. Many of these people honestly believe the government owes them a living. No one has taught them the give-to-get philosophy, so they continue taking, but not giving.

This hurts everyone, because everything the government gives away must first be taken from hard-working, tax-paying citizens like you.

William Simon, a former Secretary of the Treasury, wrote a brilliant book titled *A Time for Truth.* Here is a sample of his advice.

"Stop asking the government for 'free' goods and services, however desirable and necessary they may seem to be. They are not free. They are simply extracted from the hide of your neighbors—and can be extracted only by force. If you would not confront your neighbor and demand his money at the point of a gun to solve every new problem that may appear in your life, you should not allow the government to do it for you. Be prepared to identify any politician who simultaneously demands your 'sacrifices' and offers you 'free services' for exactly what he is: an egalitarian demagogue. This one insight understood, this one discipline acted upon and taught by millions of Americans to others could do more to further freedom in American life than any other."

People who want to get but don't want to give in return are thieves. And when the number of getters exceeds the number of givers, then our society as we know it will surely collapse. The wisdom contained in the statements, "give if you want to get," and "reward should be

---

[1] William E. Simon, *A Time for Truth,* (New York: Reader's Digest Press/ McGraw-Hill Book Company, 1978), p. 237.

earned directly by performance" are easily within the understanding of a nine-year-old.

The real enemy we face is not waiting to push a few buttons that will blow us away. The villain that can destroy us is the egalitarian demagogue Simon refers to. Giving people something for no effort expended is our greatest danger.

## Five Special Gift-Giving Techniques That Make More for You

There is an art to selecting and giving gifts. Study—then apply—the techniques suggested below. They'll make gift giving far more fun and rewarding, too.

*Rule 1: The most powerful gifts are intangible.* A phone call to a lonely person, a personal visit to a sick friend, a handwritten note saying thanks for a favor—these gifts carry far greater impact than a bunch of flowers, a standardized greeting card, or a basket of fruit. The intangible gifts suggest, "I really do care about you." The common store-bought gifts, on the other hand, say, "I've met my obligation to remember you."

*Rule 2: When you give a tangible gift, tailor it to the receiver's interest.* Each gift we give should say, "I know you—your interests, needs, wants, and desires."

A manufacturer's agent I know has mastered this technique very well. He's observed over the years that most people are collectors. And they collect just about anything you can imagine—china, metal or clay, frogs, rabbits, birds, turtles, cats, ashtrays, old thimbles—you name it and somebody collects it.

"What I do," he explained, "is keep my eyes open for unusual variations of what my customers and their spouses like to collect. When I come across something I think ties in with my customers' collecting interest, I buy it, send it to them with a brief note—something like, 'Hope this fits your collection!'

"I've found," he went on, "that I really enjoy helping build my customers' collections. Nobody who is a serious collector ever throws an item away, and they always remember who gave it to them. Besides, I've also learned that a well-chosen gift is much more appreciated than liquor, a fruit basket, or some other gift that requires no thought—only money—to buy."

The tailor-the-gift-to-the-person-who-receives-it technique works in all situations. Grandparents much prefer to receive something a grandchild made than something the child bought in a store. Most women prefer to receive flowers a friend picked in a garden than a dozen roses impersonally selected and delivered by a commercial florist. And most neighbors would rather receive a pie or cake you made than one you had a bakery deliver.

The point: Tailor your gifts to the interest of the receivers. And add your personal touch to every gift you give.

*Rule 3: Put thought value, not money value, into your gift.* Here is a valid generalization. There is no relationship between how much you spend for a gift and how much it is appreciated. People respect a gift in terms of how much thought you—the giver—put into it. Let me explain. Several years ago, I gave a talk before a large group of distributors. During the middle of the presentation, something unusual happened. (I say unusual because in more than four thousand presentations to all kinds of groups nothing like this had ever happened before.) After I had made the key point, a woman seated in the middle of this large audience got up and said, "Dr. Schwartz, I want to give you a gift for what you've done for me." For a moment, I was off-guard, but I said, "Great. I'd love to have it."

The lady then made her way to the podium and gave

me a hand-made red, white, and blue sixteen- by twenty-four-inch banner. Its caption, "In God We Trust," was superimposed above the American flag.

Today, years later, that banner is on my office wall, and I see it several times a day. The materials in the gift cost very little. And the workmanship is far from perfect. But the thought and work behind it is what counts. Chances are that gift would not bring five dollars at a flea market. But to me, it is priceless. The wonderful woman who gave me the banner knew the kind of gift I would appreciate and she had put thought and her personal effort into creating it. That's an example of a gift that wins lifetime appreciation.

*Rule 4: Give when it's least expected.* Just about everyone expects to receive gifts at Christmas, on their birthdays, on their wedding anniversary, and maybe Valentine's Day. We expect gifts on those occasions.

And because the gifts are expected, they are often not appreciated, but are taken for granted and leave no deep imprint on the receiver's mind. Often they do not convey what a true gift should: "I care about you; I'm thinking of you; I want to add to your pleasure; I want to share some of my good fortune with you."

Now the truly powerful gift is one that comes as a surprise to the receiver. A friend of mine uses this gift-giving approach very effectively. He told me, "Sure, I give at Christmas and the other appropriate times, but I also send small presents to my friends when there is absolutely no reason for them to expect a gift. I travel a lot, and when I see an item that is just right for a friend, I buy it and send it. The unexpected gift has far greater impact."

"How do you know the unexpected gift has greater influence?" I asked.

"That's easy. Most of the gifts I give at expected times never even receive a thank you, unless, of course, I hand the present to the receiver. But the unexpected gifts are almost always acknowledged with a really pleasant phone call or note.

"You see," my friend went on, "we worry about spoiling our kids with too many presents. But the problem with spoiling both kids and adults is that we bunch our giving only at certain times. One critical key to giving is to give when you want to, not when you're expected to."

*Rule 5: Give more of you. Make the second effort.* One amazing fact is the very small difference in performance between the extraordinarily successful and successful people. Consider football. The running back who averages five yards per carry is successful—he's good. But Mr. Five Yards may receive two or three times the pay and acclaim as Mr. Four Yards. What's the difference? Skill? Not really. Luck? Absolutely not. Size? No. Experience? No.

The difference is that Mr. Five Yards consistently, deliberately, and consciously on every play makes what Vince Lombardi called the second effort. He puts that "little bit more" into every play. That's the difference between being good and being excellent.

Physicians, engineers, salespeople, lawyers, managers—people in every field—can become extraordinary performers just by giving a little more of themselves to the work at hand.

What does "put a little more into it" mean? I asked three extraordinarily successful salespeople what it means to them.

A steel salesman who travels the entire nation told me, "It means making absolutely certain I know exactly what the customer needs. Then I can build my presentation to meet those specific requirements."

A wholesale furniture salesperson explained, "The second effort in my case is spending extra time teaching the retailer's salespeople how to resell the product. Few of my competitors do. That's my secret weapon."

And a salesperson for office computers explained he gave the extra difference-making effort by thinking of additional, unusual ways to use his computer in the prospect's business. "Even if the additional use is not needed now, it helps excite the prospect and the sale is easier," he explained.

Try it. Whatever you're doing, put 10 percent more into it. Join the extraordinary achievers. It means more fun and more dollars.

Let the give-to-get technique work for you. Here's how:

- Remember that generous people win; selfish people lose.
- First-class service brings first-class rewards. Second-class service leads to failure.
- Base rewards to other people on how well they perform.
- To get a lot, give a lot.
- Adapt the Kennedy quote to all your activities: Ask not what others can do for you, ask instead what can you do for them.
- Keep in mind that respect is the most treasured gift of all.
- Practice five special gift-giving techniques:
    a) Give intangible gifts whenever possible.
    b) Tailor the gift to the receiver's interests.
    c) Put thought value, not money value, into your gift.
    d) Give when it's least expected.
    e) Give more of you. Make the second effort.
- Practice this truism: It is better to give than to receive.

# 6

# How to Influence Others to Get More of What You Want

Over the past two years I have surveyed more than sixty-six hundred people on two critically significant questions. These people come from all walks of life—laborers, salespeople, managers, programmers, teachers, mechanics, truck drivers. And they represent all levels of education, different ages, ethnic backgrounds, and geographical areas of the United States and Canada.

The two questions I asked in an absolutely anonymous fashion were:

1. Do you receive as much praise, approval, and appreciation on your job as you feel you deserve?
2. Would you likely perform your job better if you received more praise, approval, and appreciation?

The answers may amaze you as much as they did me: 97.2 percent of the people answered no to question 1, and 98.4 percent answered yes to question 2.

In other words, almost all the survey respondents said they would do better work if they received more praise, appreciation, and other forms of ego satisfaction.

The White House and government officials worry about low productivity. Business executives are worried about low profits, inability to compete, and lack of initiative. You and I are concerned about how we can get better cooperation from our customers, employees, and family. How can we get other people to help us win our goals of more joy, happiness, peace of mind, friends, and money?

I've discovered the answer is simple to state. But it's tricky to implement. The solution, in three words, is *cure psychological malnutrition.* This disease, so widespread it goes almost unnoticed, costs our economy hundreds of billions of dollars each year. And most people could easily double or triple their incomes by teaching themselves to feed other people psychological nourishment instead of psychological poison.

To cure psychological malnutrition and reap big benefits in return, it is helpful to understand three concepts: the ego, ego food, and ego poison. Let me explain them briefly.

*The ego.* Your ego is your *self.* It is the most personal, most self-oriented part of your mind. Your ego is your underlying spiritual substance or soul and regulates your mental state and self-esteem. Your ego shapes and modifies your attitude toward yourself and toward other people. Your ego directs your response to every action of other people directed toward you. It is by far the most sensitive part of your psychological and philosophical structure. A broken arm may be healed in weeks; a damaged ego may never be cured.

*Ego food* is mental nourishment that makes you feel better about yourself. It enlarges your sense of self-worth, makes you feel important, useful, and needed. Ego food takes the forms of praise, encouragement, appreciation, and respect. Ego food is found in sincere statements such as:

"Mary, you handled that customer like a real pro."

"I'm really proud of you, John, for getting that shipment out on time."

"You've got a great family, Carol. You should take

pride in how well you're caring for your children."

"Fred, I appreciate your giving up your weekend—it helped us get back on schedule."

Now contrast ego food with ego poison.

*Ego poison* is the direct opposite of ego food. Ego poison consists of comments and actions of others that make you feel self-depreciated, unimportant, useless, "bad," "stupid," and "small." Comments such as the following are examples of ego poison:

"Harry, any time you want to quit, go ahead. You'd be easy to replace with someone much more competent."

"Jim, please try to not make a fool of yourself this evening. You embarrassed the heck out of me at our last party."

"Jerry, your performance in class is awful! Shape up or I'll have to set you back a grade."

"You said you'd pick me up at eight P.M. It's eight forty-five. Why don't you keep your promises?"

Now before we look at some specific ways to feed ego food and cure psychological malnutrition, let's see what general results follow when we feed people ego food and when we feed them ego poison.

*What happens when we feed ego food.* Ego food, sincerely dispensed, helps you make sales, win employee cooperation, gain love and support from people closest to you—in short, succeed.

*What happens when you feed ego poison.* Ego poison always leads to negative results. Feed ego poison and customers won't do business with you; employees deliberately goof off, take sick leave, and quit; your mate gets even with you; and your kids rebel. We know that ego poison is the number-one cause of problems at work, broken friendships, and quarrels. It's hard to believe, but it is true: Ego poison is the number-one cause of physical violence and murder!

In the work, home, and community environments, people perform second-rate because they are fed ego poison. They are scorned, overlooked, belittled, taunted, or punished. As a result, they defend their egos by acting the role of saboteurs. What people want and what will improve their performance in everything they do is praise, encouragement, rewards, appreciation, and positive reinforcement.

Let me explain how you can command more influence over others and gain more of what you want. We know that our success is determined by what we cause other people to do. Now here are two experiments, one for men and one for women. They show the results of ego food versus ego poison.

*Men, try this experiment.* Assume you are married and assume also that your wife generally makes your breakfast. Tomorrow, go to the breakfast table, pick up the plate, smell the food, and then say as insultingly as you can, "What in the heck is this? It looks awful and smells even worse." Then push yourself away from the table, take your plate to the backyard where you keep your dog, scrape the plate clean, return to the table, slam it down, and tell your wife, "I can't eat this slop. I'm going to get some breakfast on my way to work."

Now do that tomorrow morning. What kind of breakfast will you have the next day? Chances are, if you're lucky, you'll be out there with your dog! That's what feeding ego poison will do.

Another approach is this. Go to the breakfast table and say something like, "Gee, honey, this breakfast sure looks good, and you do, too." When you're finished, say something like, "You really fix me a good breakfast; it sets me up all day. And you know something else? My buddies at work, Charles and Fred, they tell me their wives don't even get up in the morning. But you do and I really appreciate it."

If you do that tomorrow morning, you will get a better breakfast the next day. (Cynics will say you will get the same breakfast. But, please, don't listen to cynics. You'll never meet one who is successful.)

The result of feeding your mate ego food will be an even greater effort on her part to please you.

*Women, try this experiment.* Let's assume you want your husband to do a special chore for you this Saturday, in this case clean out the carport and storage area. When he's finished, inspect his work and give him some ego poison. Tell him something like, "This looks awful! Why didn't you arrange things the way I told you? And there's still a trace of oil where your car is parked. That eight-year-old kid from across the street could have done a better job."

Now do that this Saturday. What will be your husband's reaction the next time you want the carport straightened out? Chances are he'll say no, tell you he has an urgent meeting he must attend, or tell you to clean it out yourself in less than polite language.

Feed him ego poison and worse results are guaranteed.

Now let's assume he doesn't clean up the carport and storage area the way you had in mind. Try some ego food. Tell him, "Bill, thanks a lot for taking care of this nasty chore. It looks great! But help me to move these boxes over there. I'll get some solvent for that grease where the car is parked."

Follow this procedure when you want some extra duty from your husband (or anyone else) and you'll get it cheerfully and enthusiastically. After a few such statements, chances are he'll come around volunteering to help.

## Why Do People Unionize?

A close associate and I have served as management consultants to many firms over a twenty-five-year period. The most common problem we are asked to help solve is stated something like this: "We're a good, reputable company. We pay our workers the prevailing wage in the area and give them the usual fringe benefits. But we just learned that some union organizers are trying to sign up our employees. And frankly, from the grapevine, we hear a majority of the workers may decide to join. We want you to help us prevent that."

In most cases, it is easy to understand why many managements don't want to have a union. Unions mean more red tape, more compliance with laws and regulations, more complicated decision making, lowered productivity, and less employee loyalty.

What many managers do not realize is that the motivation for unionizing today is not the same as in the old days. Unions still demand higher wages, shorter hours, and benefits. But the real reasons people look to unions now are psychological in nature. In a nutshell, employees want more ego food, more recognition as individuals, more acknowledgment of the importance of their jobs, and often a chance to participate in the decision-making process. Lack of respect, fair play, and honest appreciation for what they do are the real reasons employees regard managers as opponents instead of leaders.

My associate and I are able to help some companies from becoming unionized, but only when senior management makes a complete commitment to what we call a "psychological nourishment program."

Let me give you an example. Two years ago, the management of a textile company employing five hundred production workers contacted us.

The senior manager soon explained the problem. "We've been good to our people since my grandfather founded the company sixty years ago," he said. We pay them the national average for the work they do. But now, a few agitators are stirring up trouble and are talking up the union."

After some probing, my associate and I discovered that there was indeed a lot of worker discontent. With the approval of management and with extreme discretion, we interviewed twenty-five of the rank-and-file employees. Typical of the comments we heard were:

"I'm not as important as the machines I work with. One of them broke down a few months ago and they flew in a part to fix it in eight hours. When I broke my arm and was out for six weeks, nobody even called to find out how I was doing."

"Last month I had to work two double shifts [sixteen hours straight] three days in a row to get an order out on time, and my superior never even thanked me for the extra effort."

Another worker commented, "I saw how they treated John when he retired after thirty-six years in the plant. All his superior did was take an inventory of the tools assigned to him to be sure he wasn't stealing anything. They found a small tool worth about eleven dollars missing and they made him pay for it."

Further investigation convinced us that the first-line supervisors treated the employees like lepers, and the upper-level managers stayed as far away physically and psychologically as they could from the work force.

We explained to the senior manager and his associates that a five-point plan was needed—a plan that, if implemented, would not only remove the growing desire to unionize but would result in increased productivity, less absenteeism, reduced turnover, and far greater loyalty to the company.

"Sounds too good to be true," the senior manager commented. "I don't believe in miracles, but go ahead and explain your plan."

So we presented our "cure."

*Step 1.* Have all supervisors take a six-session program we had seen work many times before based on "positive supervision." We pointed out that virtually every contact supervisors now had with employees was a put down of some kind. Our job is to show supervisors how to build employees up, not tear them down.

*Step 2.* All six senior managers should be physically visible in the plant at least once a day. The visibility should include as many "hellos" and "how are you doings" as possible. The reason for manager visibility is that it unites labor and management. It makes people think "we"—not "them versus us."

*Step 3.* A personal reward system must be developed. For each department, select an employee of the month. And be sure his or her name is prominently featured on the bulletin board. We include this step because people crave—are absolutely starving for—recognition.

*Step 4.* Help the employees set up a nine-member advisory board that will report directly to senior management monthly on what can be done to make the company a better place to work. The purpose of this recommendation is to give employees a chance to participate in matters that affect them.

*Step 5.* Pay more attention to the personal desires of the work force. Remember their birthdays. If they are out sick for more than two days, phone them. Offer help when they get into trouble. Our goal here is to recognize workers as individuals—not just as numbers in the computer.

A little to our surprise, the senior manager bought our plan. About a year after the plan went into effect, he called and told us how things had improved. I said to him, "You'll recall our main assignment was to help prevent the union from getting a foothold. Did the plan do that?"

The manager laughed and said, "It sure did. Now you couldn't pay these people to join a union. They're beginning to like their work."

"That's great to hear," I responded.

"Want to know something else?" he asked. "Not only are the workers a lot happier, the supervisors and managers are, too. Production is up, costs are down, and we're becoming one big happy family."

## Admire People's Intelligence and Watch Them Support You More

Imagine for a moment you are attending a business conference. Unknown to you, three devices are attached to your body: one to measure your blood pressure, another to take your pulse, and a third to analyze the chemical content of your saliva.

The chairperson asks you for your views on how to increase sales or reduce costs or solve another problem. You make your suggestion and the chairperson looks at you angrily and says, "Your idea is too stupid to even discuss. You're paid to think. Why don't you try it sometime?"

Now, even before the chairperson had finished this remark—in no more than one second, the person monitoring your blood pressure, heartbeat, and saliva would have noted dramatic and negative reactions.

But if the chairperson had said, "Your idea may have merit. Will you take a minute or two to explain it further?," the person checking your body reactions would note good, positive medical responses.

Please note that the body responds physically to each psychological impulse. (Think about a really sour grapefruit for a moment or two and see if just thinking about it doesn't make your mouth water!) The point is that when we feed a mind ego poison, we are poisoning the body, too.

Possibly nothing does more to harm people physically than being put down psychologically. Let me give you two examples.

Wilma S. came to see me about a problem she had with her husband. Wilma explained, "It doesn't make any difference what I do, Charlie makes me feel dumb. He does everything he can to make me look stupid."

I asked Wilma to be more specific. "Well," she went on, "last weekend we had some friends over for brunch. One of the things I fixed was some stuffed eggs. Then Charlie couldn't resist telling the guests, 'There are one hundred ways to fix eggs, but Wilma hasn't learned the first one yet. Sorry if you can't digest them.' Then he took delight in saying, 'The bathroom is right down the hall.'

"It's that sort of thing all the time. Charlie lets me know I don't know how to keep house as well as his mother (although I work full time), he tells me I act silly, he pokes fun at the clothes I wear, he just never has anything good to say to or about me."

"What are you doing about it?" I asked.

"Well, there's not much I can do. As you'd expect, we quarrel a lot. I told him last night, 'Either stop making me feel I'm an idiot or I'm leaving.'"

I saw Wilma five months later. "I left Charlie shortly after you and I talked," she said. "Charlie didn't like that at all. But he had the courage to talk to our minister a number of times. I don't know exactly what the minister told him, but we're back together again. There's been a dramatic change in Charlie's attitude toward me. He brags about me at home, in public, everywhere. He makes me feel like I'm the world's smartest woman. And I love him for it."

What the counselor had done, of course, was explain to Charlie that if he wants Wilma's love, respect, and devotion, he's got to praise her for being an intelligent, capable woman, and not make her feel like an idiot.

Now here is a rule you must follow if you want other people to do more good things for you: Praise every person you deal with for their ideas, suggestions, and intelligence. Do this and you'll gain their cooperation, loyalty, and support.

Your kids want to hear, "Your homework looks great. Keep it up." Your mate loves to hear, "You're the cleverest person I've ever met."

An employee performs better when you say, "Keep coming up with ideas. You've got a good head on your shoulders."

Your customers buy more when you tell them, "Your idea for that special sale is terrific! It's certain to increase customer traffic."

Should you decide to ignore the "praise people for their intelligence rule," expect to have fewer friends, less income, little respect, and a lot less satisfaction.

The cynics you know may laugh at you for being stupid and following the "praise for their intelligence" rule. But feel sorry for them. If putting other people down is what "satisfies" them, let them enjoy falling further and further behind.

## How to Use Four Varieties of Ego Nourishment to Get Positive Let-Me-Help-You Action

To influence other people to buy from you, work harder for you, and help you get what you want requires more than just knowing that feeding ego food is a good idea. You have to put the theory in practice. Here are four specific varieties of soul nutrition you can use every day to help you influence others.

*1. Praise people for what their family is and does.* To many people, the most important part of their lives is their family. Parents appreciate you when you make a comment like, "You must be really proud of Jimmy. I saw him score that winning goal," or "Janet looks just wonderful in her ballerina costume."

Ask older parents about their children—where they live, what they are doing, their grandchildren, their plans for the future, and you will be making friends fast.

Note of caution: Always be sure the conversation focuses on the other person's kids, spouse, parents, and other relatives—not yours! Resist with all your might the desire to tell how great your family is. When other people talk about families, most of us play a game of "top it" or, by implication, tell the other person, "Members of my family are really better than yours." You never win friends that way. Simply talk in terms of other people's interests, not yours, and you'll win the influence you want.

*2. Praise people for the job they do.* This kind of ego food is exceptionally potent for two reasons. (a) It is seldom used, and (b) people love it. A newspaper reporter told me why she got a job with another paper. "In two years with the *Chronicle,* I covered a lot of stories. But not once did the editor ever tell me, 'That's a fine story,' or 'You did a good job covering so and so.' The best he could come up with was, 'The story is okay. Run it.'"

I have met carpenters, truck drivers, supervisors, janitors, managers, people from almost every conceivable occupation who have told me, "I can't remember when my superior told me I was doing a good job."

It is terrible to think about. Next to the family, work is the most important part of people's lives.

Why do some people avoid praising others for the work they do? The president of a computer-programming firm asked me to talk to one of his managers. He commented, "Technically, Linda B. is well qualified. But she's negative with her personnel. Perhaps a discussion with you will put her on the right track."

I asked the manager of the programming group who had a reputation for never praising her people why she followed that policy.

"I think I know your philosophy about feeding ego food to employees, but I don't buy it," she began, "and I've got three good reasons. First, if I told my people they're doing a good job, they would slack off and do a poorer job. Complimenting them for the work they do would not produce more good programs, but it would produce more absenteeism and more nonessential conversation. Second," she went on, "sometimes my programmers don't do their work well. Now if you praise people for second-rate performance, you're certain to get third-rate performance."

"What's your third reason for not complimenting your people for their work?" I asked.

"Just this," she replied. "If I pass out ego food as you suggest, my people will start hounding me for better pay, more time off, easier assignments, you name it."

Linda B. and I had two in-depth discussions. Finally, quite reluctantly, Linda agreed to begin feeding some ego food to her staff. Before long, she discovered what she called a miracle. "As I began to pass out praise, I found my people cooperating better, enjoying their work, and producing more. Much to my surprise, your formula works."

I thanked Linda for having the courage to try the build-people-up approach, since many managers are afraid to practice praising people for the work they do.

Then Linda added, "Know something else? The fears I had that my people would demand more pay, easier assignments, more free time—those sorts of things—just didn't materialize. Since I've started showing real appreciation for what my people do, they're actually volunteering for extra assignments. I confess, you've made a believer out of me."

*3. People love you when you tell them they look great.* Few things encourage people more than to be told they look great! This is because of all the things people worry and feel self-conscious about the most is the way they look.

The desire to look good helps explain the enormous popularity of weight-reduction programs, jogging, tennis, and other health-conditioning activities. "I want to look better" is also the backbone of the apparel industry. Face-lifting and body remodeling are billion-dollar enterprises because people want to be perceived as handsome, beautiful, young, and attractive.

A friend of mine has been the executive director of a large trade association for fifteen years. He told me recently as we lunched that many of the people he knew when he became head of the association at age thirty-five are now getting up in years. He explained to me how difficult it is to keep peace at the annual conventions when the industry leaders want to bicker over changes they perceive as important.

"Like getting rid of you?" I asked.

"Exactly," he laughed. "Our members are a bunch of

fine people, and I've discovered a little technique that helps keep them giving me their support."

"What's that?" I asked. Having worked with hundreds of trade associations over the years, I was curious.

"Just this. When I greet each of them for the first time at a meeting, I tell him or her how great they look. And I do more than just generalize. I take note of weight loss, suntans, clothes, those sorts of things—and they love it.

"I have made it a rule," my friend went on, "that I comment favorably on the appearance of everyone I meet on a one-to-one basis. It simply works great when you notice a woman's hair or jewels or tell some guy how much you admire his vest or sport jacket or shoes.

"You see," he said, "I make it a point to look for things I can admire in another person's appearance. Most people either don't notice anything special about how another person looks or they're too jealous to say anything."

Praise people for the way they look and it makes them feel better physically, too. Here is an important point: You can help make other persons well or sick simply by telling them they look good or bad. All conversation is to some extent hypnotic. Let me explain. For many years, I played a game in group training situations to illustrate this point. At random, I'd select someone who looked young and perfectly healthy. In the middle of a presentation, I'd go to the targeted person and tell him he looked sick. Then I'd elaborate and mention that his color was greenish and he looked like he might soon vomit. In just seconds, the fellow would look sick and ask to be excused. I finally stopped doing this when a fellow fainted.

Now, since you can literally make someone ill with suggestions of how bad they look, doesn't it also follow that you can help make someone well by suggesting how good they look? It may seem like a small point, but put it to use just the same. In persuasive psychology, little things make a big difference. When you meet an old friend or a new one, tell them how good they look ("Jane, I don't know how you do it, but every time we meet, I swear you've gotten younger", or "Bill, what's your formula for staying so trim?").

*4. Praise people for what they own and miracles happen.* Ask yourself, "What is the main reason people buy things?" To survive? Not really. Increasingly, people take the necessities of life for granted.

A key reason—often the main reason—for buying new clothes, cars, furniture, houses, and a host of other things is the desire to win approval of others.

You see, we live in a pragmatic world. Success is judged in part by what one owns. All of us desire success. It follows then that people crave admiraton for what they acquire. A few people deny this, but don't let their denials fool you. A friend I know is very anti-materialistic, but he takes great pride in the placques he has acquired over the years and the new car the community leaders gave him for his untiring service to the city. People do want to own more and they do want admiration from you for what they own.

Knowing that people take pride in their possessions is a clue to helping you acquire more. Let me give you an example.

A car salesman I know, Larry M., is, year in and year out, the top producer for a large General Motors dealership. I've watched him sell on many occasions and it's always an artistic experience. Usually, when people buy a new car, they trade in an old one. And typically the new car salesperson will have the appraiser put a value on the old car. But not Larry M. First, he appraises the car with the appraiser. This greatly increases Larry's credibility in the mind of the prospect. Second, after the value in the trade-in is set, Larry compliments the prospect on how well the trade-in has been cared for, the many miles it still has left, and so on. Larry avoids what most car salespeople do—telling the customer what bad shape the old car is in and why it's worth so little in a trade for a new car.

"Actually," Larry explained to me, "the value I put on a trade-in is just about the same as any other salesperson. In the final analysis, supply and demand plus competiton fixes the price we can offer for a trade-in. But the customers like to hear positve comments on the trade-in. It's been their friend for several years. Inside their heads, they want to know that I appreciate that old friend."

Another person I know, Adam S., sells home improvements. And he's a superstar. Adam follows essentially the same pattern as Larry M. "As I inspect a home to see what repair or remodeling services I can offer, I admire different things the prospect owns—maybe an aquarium, an antique of some kind—anything I think the prospect takes great pride in owning." Adam explains, "You see, when I praise them for what they own, I am admiring their intelligence and judgment. People love that. And showing respect for what people already have makes my job of selling home improvements a whole lot easier."

Next time you visit someone's home, praise him for one or two specific objects. When someone buys a new car or house or boat, let him know how much you admire it.

Avoid with all the power you have the human inclination to be jealous and put down your friend's new possession. Remember, people love to be praised for what they are able to acquire. Give them the praise they want and they will help you get what you want.

## Praise by Listening and Make Friends in the Process

One of the most effective techniques for influencing other people is extraordinarily simple. Just listen to what they want to tell you. People want to talk about two things: first, what they have achieved (brag a little), and second, their problems (complain a little).

Other people find joy in telling you about their interests, how advanced their children are, their achievements, their possessions, and their plans for the future. People love to talk about themselves, and as often as possible.

The second thing people want to talk about, although usually in private, is their problems. People feel a real need to tell someone about their bad luck, how they have been mistreated, how awful their marriage partner is, their boss's misbehavior, their business partner or some other person who took advantage of them, how the IRS or other government agency nailed them—things of that sort.

Whether people want to brag or complain, listen to them. Here's why.

The people you meet will think you are a great conversationalist when you let them tell you about the books they've read, the places they've visited, the famous people they know, and their plans for the future. If you do most of the talking, the other person will consider you a bore.

And when people want to bring you their problems, listen and they will think you are wise, understanding, and helpful. Never, absolutely never, tell them your problems.

When you do talk in conversation, say as little as possible. A sign of great people is the ability to refrain from a lot of talk, and when they do talk, they say a lot in a few words. Learn a lesson from Calvin Coolidge, our President between 1923 and 1928.

Observe how much Calvin Coolidge could say in just a few words:

"The business of America is business."

"If you don't say anything, you won't be called on to repeat it."

"Collecting more taxes than is absolutely necessary is legalized robbery."

"No person was ever honored for what he received. Honors have always been rewards for what people give."

Much of "Silent Cal" Coolidge's quiet success as President was that he encouraged other people to talk and then listened to what they had to say.

## We Stress Talking and Neglect Listening

One fault in our educational system is that too much emphasis is placed on how to speak and too little on how to listen. Courses in speaking are taught everywhere. Books about how to speak would fill a library. Yet there is little to read or hear about the techniques and research of effective listening.

## How Listening Won a Politician a Seat in Congress

A friend of mine explained how he used the listen-to-people's-problems technique to win his first election.

"Most politicians," he observed, "go to the people with a platform—a cut-and-dried formula for solving what they, the candidates, perceive to be what people want done. But being awfully naive and not too sure I really knew what the voters wanted, I used a different approach. I organized my whole campaign around the idea, 'Bring me your problems; I'll work to solve them.' In shopping centers, town meetings, talk shows, debates, everywhere I went, I asked the voters to tell me their problems. And with all my might, I resisted proposing immediate solutions and giving pat answers.

"You wouldn't believe the problems people told me about: 'Can you help get my son's prison term reduced?'; 'My daughter is going blind and we can't afford the laser surgery that's needed'; 'The IRS says I owe them money but I don't'; 'The court won't let me visit my child'; 'My tenants are tearing up my property and yet they laugh at me when I try to collect rent.'

"I collected literally thousands of problems. And as often as possible, I'd get the names and addresses of people who told me what help they wanted. Then, just a few days before the election, my staff and I wrote each person a thank-you note for telling us his or her problem with a promise from me that I'd go to work on it when I was elected.

"As you know," my friend continued, "I was elected by a good majority. The fact that I'm still in the Congress proves I've been doing all I can directly and indirectly to solve what the people see as their problems— not what I think they are."

People—all of them—citizens, customers, employees, family members, neighbors—want to talk. Let them, and you're on your way to gaining their confidence in you.

## Listening Works in Business, Too

Most marketing organizations hold annual sales meetings. And typically, the home-office executives get together well in advance of the meeting to map out plans for making next year even better. So far, so good. The difficulty with this approach is that often the people who do the planning don't know what the real problems are. As a result, next year's marketing effort produces less than the desired results.

A marketing manager for an apparel firm I know uses the listen-to-the-troops approach and gets great results. Here's how he goes about it. About a month before the annual sales meeting, he phones each sales representative and asks him or her what the company can do to help them sell more next year (and in the process, make more money). "I find this technique enormously effective. I get ideas about pricing, promotion, what lines to stress or de-stress.

"Most sales meetings," he went on, "are like classes in high school. The sales manager (the teacher) gets before the group and lays down the law. Here are the dos and don'ts, the rights and the wrongs. And this is how we (the teacher and his staff) have decided to handle the them.

"Our approach is different. We get the real problems our representatives face and together we find solutions. And our reps don't mind following the plans, because they participated in making them.

"You have no idea," my friend went on, "how many good ideas people on the firing line have about how to do a better marketing job."

## Listening to People Is Making Thomas B. Prosperous

Thomas B. specializes in selling tax-deferred pension plans to educators. And he's very successful. I've known Thomas for about five years. One day I asked Thomas why he was doing so well when at least five other companies sold and serviced plans that were as good as his. His answer was simple: "I listen—then I act.

"You see," he explained, "my business is basically investing some of your income so you won't have to pay taxes on it—and on what the money earns—until you retire. Well, everyone's situation is different—it involves a spouse, children, insurance, outside earnings—a lot of things that are as confidential, maybe more so, than what you tell your physician. Sometimes government policy gets involved, tax rulings—all sorts of things. I listen to what my clients have to say and then I make my recommendations. I do more business on this campus than my four competitors combined."

"But there must be more to your diagnostic technique than you've told me," I said.

"Well, a couple of things," Thomas added. "Everything I learn about a client's personal or professional problems I keep absolutely confidential." Then he looked at me and said, "You know at least fifteen or twenty of my clients. Have I ever breathed a word to you about their personal affairs—income, pending divorces, debts, things like that?"

I said, "No, you haven't. I had never thought of it, but you have never once gossiped with me about other people."

"There's something else, too," Thomas went on. "I never talk about my personal problems, my politics, or my religion."

Then Thomas asked me, "Do you know whom I voted for in the last election?"

I said, "No."

"Do you know how many kids I have, their ages, what they are doing?"

Again, I had to admit I didn't know.

Thomas went on, "A key principle of success I've discovered is, let other people talk about themselves, their problems, their families, their goals, and don't talk about yours."

Thomas made three excellent points: (a) encourage people to talk, (b) keep sensitive information other people tell you confidential, and (c) talk as little as possible about yourself.

## How to Deal with Put-Downers Successfully

After discussing positive ways to influence others, someone will say to me, "If your ideas work so well and are so powerful, why don't my superiors use them on me? I receive a lot more criticism than praise in my work."

I have two answers to that observation. First, a lot of people—most people, in fact—are simply ignorant of the power of ego food and how to use it. They have yet to learn that praise, not punishment, gets results. They do not understand what President Lincoln meant when he said, "A drop of honey will attract more bees than a gallon of gall."

The second answer to the comment, "Other people don't praise me, so why should I praise them?" is very practical. "Your success," I suggest, "is based on what you cause other people to do—buy from you, work harder for you, love you, and support you. If other people want to use the put-others-down technique, that's their business. They're wrong, but they make the choice. Do what works. Keep on feeding ego food and enjoy the rewards it brings."

It is sad but very true: There are people who take devilish delight in seeing you make a mistake, look bad on the job, get reprimanded, or make a blunder of some kind. Chances are you've been around put-downers as long as you can remember. Even in this enlightened age, some children, usually following the example of their parents, enjoy making fun of another child.

The problem is that most people would rather criticize and find fault with you than praise you or compliment you for what you are, do, contribute, or achieve.

Can't is not a common word in my vocabulary, but it must be used here. You can't escape the put-downers, but you can take good cheer in knowing that a direct correlation exists between how much one is criticized and that person's degree of success. The most criticized person in the nation is usually the President; in your company, it's the chief executive officer; in a school, it is either the principal or the football coach.

Granted, being put down accompanies success. But how do we deal with it? Here are four recommendations:

*1. Accept criticism as proof you're growing.* Because you are moving ahead, you are a threat to insecure people who, convinced that they can't equal your performance, take pot shots at you. Remember, the least criticized person in any organization is not the manager, the key salesperson, or the chief accountant. The person who is never put down, runs no job risk, and survives recessions and mergers is usually the janitor.

*2. Never fight the criticism.* When falsely accused of something, the most natural thing you want to do is fight back and set the record straight. Don't. As Shakespeare wrote so carefully in *Hamlet,* Act III, "The lady doth protest too much methinks," meaning than when we strongly profess our innocence we look more and more guilty. One little example illustrates this point. Let's assume you buy a pair of shoes. A put-downer in front of other people may say, "I saw a pair just like your shoes at Joe's Discount Shoes [the cheapest store in town], marked down fifty percent." Now, if you try to explain that you bought the shoes at a high-quality store and you paid a good price for them, the bystanders will begin to believe the put-downer because you are protesting too much. Simply ignore the put-downer and immediately people will recognize him for what he is—a small, petty, jealous put-downer. Follow this suggestion and you'll win in situations like these.

The pragmatic philosopher Elbert Hubbard once said, "To escape criticism—do nothing, say nothing, be nothing."

*3. Feel sorry for those who put you down.* This sounds like a tall order, but it's needed so you can keep the small hates aimed your way in perspective. The professional put-downers, the folks who find fault with everyone and everything, are sick. Your critics are envious, jealous, and filled with self-hate. Remember the example of Jesus at his crucifixion: "Forgive them, Father, for they know now what they do."

Think about that observation the next time someone tries to make you look bad at work, embarrasses you at a party, or tells lies about you hoping to get you in trouble. In the final analysis and over time, put-downers put themselves down even further. Feel genuinely sorry for those troublemakers who want to hurt you. Their behavior suggests they are sick.

## How Does Punishment Fit Into My Plans for Achieving More?

Often people who sincerely want to be winners ask me, "But some people deserve to be punished. How do I deal with them?"

Well, there are two kinds of crime: Breaking the law as written by man and breaking the spiritual law. Now it's the job of law-enforcement people to deal with man-written laws. In passing, there isn't much agreement as to how best to deal with law-breaking crimes. Henry Ford observed, "Capital punishment is as fundamentally wrong as a cure for crime as charity is wrong as a cure for poverty." Meanwhile, Alexander I. Solzhenitsyn said, "When we neither punish nor reproach evildoers . . . we are ripping the foundations of justice from beneath new generations."

There is a lot of the type-one form of crime. This we know even if we don't read newspapers or watch TV. Type-two crime, breaking the laws of the spirit, is by far the more common. It happens to most of us every day.

When someone deliberately trips you, makes you look like a fool, or takes credit for what you contributed, the human inclination is to get revenge. But the "get revenge" method is wrong, always wrong.

Sooner or later, if you keep doing the best you know how, the organizational cowards who want to take credit for your creativity will be found out. A young copywriter for an advertising agency told me recently that he conceived most of the promotional ideas and wrote the copy for a very successful promotional campaign. But his boss took the credit for the campaign and for having chosen the copy ideas. The copywriter (according to the boss) may have selected a word here and there, the typeface, done those relatively menial tasks. Then the boss was out sick for five weeks, and the campaign went on even more successfully without him. It wasn't long before the department head realized who really was the brains behind the ads. In short order, the copywriter moved up and his boss moved out.

The point is this: Don't waste time and intelligence

and emotional energy trying to get revenge with those who tell lies about you, steal your ideas, or take credit for your work. Sooner or later, the people who have broken the laws of the spirit are themselves broken by all they have done. The mills of the gods grind slowly . . .

To win more influence over others, apply these rules:

- Keep in mind that feeding people ego food wins cooperation, loyalty, and sacrifices from other people.
- Feeding people ego poison always produces negative results.
- Admire people's intelligence and you harness their mental ability for worthwhile goals.
- Remember, the body responds physically to every psychological impulse. For better health, reward people with ego food.
- At every opportunity, praise people for:
  - a) What their family is and does.
  - b) The job they do.
  - c) How good they look.
  - d) What they own.
- Listen to what others have to say and you will win friends in the process.
- Deal with people who want to put you down in a positive way. Just:
  - a) Accept criticism as proof you're growing.
  - b) Never fight back at criticism.
  - c) Feel sorry for your critics.
- Never, absolutely never, try to get revenge. It reduces you to your tormentor's level.

# 7

# Use the A.S.K. Formula to Get More

The Bible is filled with wisdom. The Golden Rule, "Do unto others the way you would have them do unto you," is the perfect guide for effective human relations. If it were practiced by everyone, we would not quarrel with our mates, take unfair advantage of others in business, steal, or have wars. Followed properly, the "do unto others the way you would have them do unto you" rule would end human conflicts.

But the Bible also contains money-making, wealth-producing proverbs and maxims. One of them, when put to daily use, is certain to help you earn a high income, accumulate beautiful objects, win respect, and acquire more influence over others.

That simple but enormously potent maxim is:

Ask, and it shall be given unto you.
Seek, and ye shall find.
Knock, and it shall be opened unto you.

Now, before you read on, take a few minutes to make a list of some of the good things you would like to have but which you have not asked for. Maybe your list will look something like this.

—A promotion to a more interesting, better-paying, more responsible job?

—A transfer to a different job or job location?

—Better cooperation from your support personnel?

—Advice on how best to pursue your career?

—More love?

—More business from your customers? More new customers? More profit?

—More fun and joy with your spouse?

—A date with someone you admire a lot?

—Help from a very prominent person?

The list of what people want is endless. As you read this chapter, keep in mind this law of achievement: Successful people are askers. They ask for what they want, and that is a basic reason why they enjoy more.

The A.S.K. formula (ask, seek, and knock) is guaranteed to get you more love, happiness, money, and success in every dimension if you will apply it. The A.S.K. concept should become so deeply a part of your subconscious that you apply it automatically at work, in your home, with friends, among strangers.

Let me share with you some examples of people who have reaped big rewards because they learned to ask.

## John S. Asked an Expert to Be His Mentor. The Payoff Was Fantastic.

It takes much more than knowledge to make money. There are, in fact, many highly knowledgeable people with college degrees who fail to find satisfaction or achieve wealth. What is needed to achieve more besides knowledge is wisdom. And wisdom takes time and is difficult to acquire. But there are shortcuts.

Recently, a business friend phoned me and asked me to have lunch with him. My friend told me a president of a medium-sized bank in Florida was in town and he would like me to meet him. "He has an unusually good mind," my friend explained. "You'll enjoy talking with him."

When I met George A., the banker, I was astonished at his youth, and my amazement showed. I apologized to George, explaining I had expected to meet someone much older.

He laughed and said, "It happens every day. I'll be thirty-three next week, and maybe I'll soon be old enough so I'll stop shocking people."

In the back of my mind, I thought a relative must be a major shareholder in the bank and had used some influence to help the young man move up so fast. But soon I learned this was not the case. The young banker had made it on his own.

I said to my new friend, "George, very few people make it to the top of a bank at such a young age. Tell me, how did you do it?"

"It took a lot of hard work and dedication," he explained, "but the real secret is that I selected a mentor."

"What do you mean by a mentor?" I asked.

"Let me explain," George continued. "During my senior year at the university, a retired banker addressed the class. He was in his seventies. His parting remark was, 'If I can ever help any of you, just call.' It sounded as though he was just being polite, but his offer intrigued me. I wanted his advice on getting off on the right foot in banking, but I confess I was nervous. After all, he was wealthy and prominent and I was only a student about to finish college. But finally, I got the courage and called him."

"What happened?" I asked.

"Frankly, I was amazed," the young banker responded. "He was very friendly and invited me to meet with him. I did and got a vault full of advice. He gave me some good pointers on how to choose a bank to work for, and then how to sell myself so I'd land a job. His parting remark to me was, 'If you want me to, I'll serve as your coach.'

"My coach and I developed an excellent relationship," George explained. "I call him at least once a week and we have a long lunch about once a month. He never tries to solve my problems for me. Rather, he helps me understand different alternatives for solving banking problems.

"And interestingly," my friend continued, "my coach is genuinely grateful to me for letting him advise me. He's now in his eighties and he told me recently that our visits keep him thinking young."

Back in my office that afternoon, my eyes focused on a motto on my wall. It says, "We need all the help we can get." How true. And the help is there if we seek it out. There are many, many highly successful people in every walk of life who stand ready to assist success-oriented people if we ask them.

Regardless of what kind of work you do, find a mentor. It will help you to maximize your ability. And chances are it will bring satisfaction to your coach, too. Remember, a well-chosen mentor can help you find shortcuts to where you want to go.

Just suppose for a moment that George had not accepted the offer of the retired banker. Chances are his move to the top of the bank would have taken at least a decade longer, or quite possibly he never would have made it.

If you can use help in your career, seek out a mentor. Someone out there is eager to help.

## Successful People Want to Help You. Ask Them.

Here is a key success concept, but it is difficult for people, especially those who are just starting their careers:

Asking someone for advice is about the sincerest

praise you can give another person. When you ask some-one for advice, you are praising that person for his knowledge, experience, and wisdom. And when you ask successful people for guidance, you'll get ideas that can help you achieve. Let me cite an example.

A friend of mine, Carl M., is extraordinarily successful in the insurance business. One evening at dinner, I asked Carl how he managed to make it to the top in his company.

I said to Carl, "I know you're intelligent, ambitious, self-directed, and you know the insurance business inside and out. But perhaps five thousand other people in your company do, too. What makes you so much more effective than the great majority of other people in your company?"

Carl thought for a moment, and then said, "David, I found a key to success that is so simple you may not believe it."

"Tell me about it," I said.

"Well, I started in the insurance business when I was twenty-eight. At the end of my first year, I was about ready to throw in the towel. I no longer had a drawing account, just straight commission. I wasn't making sales. I was depressed and angry with myself. And I resented the fact that we were living almost entirely off my wife's income. Then I got an idea. Maybe it was something I subconsciously remembered from *Think and Grow Rich,* the Napoleon Hill book.

"I decided," Carl continued, "that before I gave up, I was going to ask the most successful person in our company for his advice. That evening I called Sam W., who had been the number-one agent four years in a row.

"I admit I was really afraid to call Sam. After all, he was number one in the company and I was in the group that soon would be terminated. But I swallowed all my pride and made the call, although I had never met him personally. I explained my plight to Sam. After about a fifteen-minute conversation, Sam said, 'Look, Carl, I want to help you. Can you come to Dallas next week for a couple of days? I'll show you as many of my tactics as I can. They may not work for you, but they work wonders for me. You can at least observe the techniques I use and then give them a try.'"

"Did you go to Dallas?" I asked.

"You bet I did," Carl replied. "Instead of two days, I spent an entire week with Sam. He explained how he prospected, made appointments, handled objections, and closed sales—strictly the nuts and bolts of selling insurance.

"As we parted at the airport, Sam told me, 'Look, call me as often as you want if you think I can help.' Then he said something else, 'Carl, you're the first protégé I've ever had. I won't be satisfied until you're number one in the company.'

"For the first couple of years," Carl went on, "I'd call Sam two or three times a week. Often the conversations were very brief, two minutes or less. Sam was very quick to diagnose my problems. Month after month, my sales volume went up and I continued to stay in close touch with Sam. After all, I was his protégé and he was my mentor."

"That is a delightful case history," I observed.

"But that isn't quite all of the story," Carl said. "Three years ago, I really caught on fire and I was the number-one producer in the entire company. At the annual awards banquet, the president selected Sam to award me the plaque for being number one. In all my life, I've never seen a man weep with so much joy."

Carl paused a moment, and then, with tears in his eyes, he said, "Sam died six months ago. After the service, his widow put her arms around me and said,

'Thanks for letting Sam share his success with you. Helping you was one of the most important things in his life.'"

I've reflected on that conversation with Carl many, many times. Asking successful people for advice is a key to success. Seek advice from winners. Regardless of your field—law, medicine, selling, management, farming, religion, music, education, or what have you, choose a superstar as your model. And don't be afraid to ask for help. Here is a rule to remember: The more successful a person is, the more that person wants to share knowledge, wisdom, and experience with others who want to maximize their talents. One of the greatest joys people have is to share their good fortune with others. Successful people, you will discover, are very generous in helping others. They know the world is rich, and anyone who wants to enjoy great things can, if they really try.

## If You Want a Promotion, Ask for It

During a management seminar in Colorado several years ago, a senior plant manager, Bill S., talked with me during a coffee break. I had just finished a presentation on the subject "Personal Qualities That Lead to Promotion."

Bill said, "I agree with your criteria for promotion, but you left out one important factor. You didn't drive home the importance of an individual wanting to be promoted."

I thought for a moment and replied, "You're right. My presentation was geared to those qualities that you— a senior manager—could observe in lower-level personnel. It did not deal with the desire of lower-level people for advancement."

"Exactly," Bill went on, "and right now there are probably hundreds of thousands of managers who would qualify for and win promotions if they would do just one thing."

"What's that?" I asked.

Bill replied, "Simply ask their superiors for a promotion. They won't always get it, but asking for it sure helps."

I remembered my discussion with Bill months later when Janice R., a former student of mine, came to see me with a problem. She complained that she had not been promoted in three years. "I've seen people less qualified than I get promoted to better-paying jobs, but I've been overlooked," she explained. "And I don't think it's fair. What should I do?"

"Well," I replied, "I don't know much about your company, so I don't know whether the senior management is fair or not. But, Janice, tell me, have you asked to be promoted?"

Janice looked confused and answered, "Why, no. I haven't asked. I assume my superior knows my work is well above average."

Then, again reflecting on the lesson Bill had taught me, I explained to Janice that higher-level managers regard superior performance as important, but they want another quality in people they promote. They prefer to promote people who want to be leaders. The desire to lead is the most important part of the leadership process. When you ask for a promotion, you display initiative. And senior managers like that.

I summed up the conversation with this suggestion. "Janice, next week tell your superior you think you are qualified for promotion and that you want the responsibility that goes with it."

Janice called me several weeks later to tell me she did

ask, and she did get the promotion. That was five years ago. Since then, I've had three calls from Janice to tell me of three more promotions. In that five-year period, her income increased by 300 percent!

When you think about it, you will be amazed about all the good things in life you have not received because you did not ask.

If you believe you deserve a promotion, ask for it. There is great wisdom in the old saying, "The squeaky wheel gets the grease"—if the squeaky wheel is needed.

## Ask People, Don't Order People Around

Watch what goes on in most offices, factories, retail stores, any place where work is done. You'll observe two ways—at the extremes—that instructions are given. Boss Type A tells the people what to do:

"Jim, get this order delivered by eleven A.M., and don't be late."

"Mary, I want all these memos out by four P.M."

"Bill, one more mistake like this one and you're through."

"Sam [his child], if I don't see an A on your next report card, there goes your allowance."

Contrast Boss Type A with Boss Type B. He asks, he doesn't order or threaten.

"Jim, this delivery is real important. Can you get it delivered by eleven A.M.?"

"Mary, I don't believe we're as rushed as yesterday. Can you get this stack of memos in the interoffice mail by four o'clock? It sure would help the staff meetings get off to a good start tomorrow."

"Bill, will you call me when you have a few minutes and let me show you a way to adjust the machine?"

"Sam, I'm really glad to see you made a B this period. I'll be home all evening. Call me if I can help you with your homework. Let's try for an A next period."

Here's the point: Few people like to be ordered to do things. When you order people around, you tell them they're (a) stupid, (b) unimportant, and (c) inferior to you.

The age of the master and servant is over! Every person in an organization is important. For example, if the "unimportant" mail clerk didn't deliver the mail, imagine how fouled up a business would be in just a few hours, or if "anybody" can be a receptionist and insults visitors, the whole organization gets a black eye.

Ordering people to perform leads to less thinking, higher turnover, more pilferage, more absenteeism, more mistakes, and other negatives that lead to lowered productivity.

But when you ask people for their ideas, help, cooperation, and sacrifice, you help them identify with the company. It becomes their organization and they will perform better because they identify with what's happening. Besides, it gives them a sense of importance and pride—the indispensable ingredients in every successful organization.

## Phrase Your Questions to Get a Positive Response

When people do ask, most of them phrase their questions to get a negative response. For example, how often has someone asked you, "You don't happen to have the time, do you?" The way the question is asked calls for the answer, "No, I don't."

The proper way to ask the question is simply, "What

time is it?" Keep tabs for a few days on the questions you are asked that call for a negative answer. Examples are:

"You haven't heard if Friday will be a holiday, have you?"

"I don't suppose you'd be interested in buying that eighty-acre tract I told you about?"

"I suppose I couldn't leave a few minutes early today, could I?"

Questions asked like this usually get—and deserve—a negative reply.

Let me cite examples of three ways to ask. Some years ago, I gave a test to one of my classes. Performance was miserable, the highest grade was 73. After the scores were released, one student came to me and said, "You're not going to scale the grades, are you?" I said no.

Later, a second student came by and asked, "Are you going to scale the grades?" This time I said, "I haven't decided."

Still later, a third student asked, "How much are you going to scale the grades?"

The first student phrased his request to get a no answer. The second student's request was designed to get either a yes or a no reply. But the third student asked a question that presumed I would scale the grades. Her question took my mind off the big decision—should I scale the grades at all, and put my mind to work on how much I should scale the grades.

I've been around many salespeople who ask questions of their prospects in the same three ways the students used.

One salesperson says, "Well, from your comments I guess you don't want to place an order, do you?" One hundred percent of the time the prospect says no.

A second salesperson says, "Do you want to place an

order?" Here the answer can be yes or no, but likely will be no.

A third salesperson says, "How many units do you feel you need, twenty gross or thirty gross?" In this case, the prospect's mind is taken off the big decision—do I want to buy any units at all?—and is focused on choosing how many units to buy.

The point is simply this: Assume the other person will answer your question affirmatively, so phrase your question to get a positive answer.

## Ask Questions: It Proves You're Intelligent

It's sad but true that many people feel if they ask questions during a lecture, orientation session, around a conference table, or even in a social situation, they will look foolish and be subjected to laughter and ridicule by others who are present.

One young woman told me her own sad experience— sad because she was afraid to ask questions. "You see," she began, "I had just been hired by a bank and I was assigned to computer operations. The first step was to take a four-week course in computers. Well, I knew nothing about how computers worked, but the other people in the class did. As the course unfolded, a lot of the procedures were beyond my comprehension, but I was afraid to ask for more explanation. I didn't want to look dumb before the other employees. Well, when I was given a regular duty assignment, I made some bad mistakes and was fired in three days."

I told the young woman never to be afraid to ask for more information. And if someone should laugh or make nasty comments, feel sorry for them. Only fools laugh at ignorance. Wise people help you overcome it.

The truth is, asking questions is a sign of intelligence. Professors agree that students who ask the most questions usually receive the highest grades. Executives will tell you that support personnel who ask questions and are inquisitive move higher and faster up the organizational ladder than their counterparts who just sit and listen and pretend to understand. And top salespeople know they are not in a talker's profession—they are diagnosticians. They ask prospective customers a lot of relevant questions about the prospects' needs and requirements. Selling is, after all, a process of asking questions, evaluating the answers, and then proposing solutions.

Many people were discouraged by their parents from asking questions. Yet the main way a child develops his or her intelligence is by asking questions. But some parents are too impatient, too busy, or too selfish to help their children understand what puzzles them. The result is that many people grow up thinking it's wrong to ask.

Cement this concept in your mind right now. Asking questions proves you've got intelligence and you want to add to it. So, when in doubt, ask.

## If You Feel You've Been Wronged, Ask for Corrective Action

Many years ago, in college, I learned an interesting lesson from another student that reinforces the importance of asking. My friend, John S., and I were eating in a cafeteria one day. I said to John, "I'm a bit jealous of you. You seem to get so many breaks that the rest of us don't. For example, this quarter all the rest of us in class had to do term projects that the instructor assigned. You did one of your own choice. And last quarter you got Professor Becker to change your grade—something I'm told he never does. Even going through the cafeteria line, you ended up with a bigger piece of cherry pie than I! Why?"

John smiled and replied, "It's basically simple. I'm not afraid to ask. Let me explain. After the professor had assigned our term projects, I approached him and explained that I had a special interest in a different area and I thought I could benefit more if I wrote about the subject of my choice. The professor thought for a moment, and said, 'Go ahead. My role is that of a guide, not a dictator. Do what will benefit you most.' It was that simple."

"Now, about that grade change," John continued, "I honestly felt I had done better on the final than the professor had decided. So I simply saw the professor and asked him to reconsider. He did, and agreed I had been undergraded.

"As for the piece of cherry pie, you didn't notice that all I did was ask the guy behind the counter, very politely, if he had a slightly bigger piece, and sure enough, he found one."

Many situations come up in life when we feel we've been wronged. When that happens, ask for corrective action. But always ask for correction like a lady or gentleman. Most people who have some control over our lives will be glad to make things right if, in fact, they have wronged us. But when asking for corrective action, always be polite and businesslike. When you demand your rights, you encourage the other person to resist, to fight you, and you end up losing.

## When Asking, Don't Fear Rejection

After making a presentation some time ago on the rewards of learning to ask for what you want, a woman named Becky asked to talk to me privately. We went to a nearby coffee shop, and soon Becky began to unburden herself.

"I like what you said about asking," Becky said, "but frankly, I'm afraid to ask. I dislike rejection so much, I'd rather do without something than ask for it and be told I can't have it."

"Why do you think you have this fear?" I asked. "Do you think it may have something to do with your childhood?"

Becky looked surprised and replied, "I hadn't thought my problem might relate to my childhood, but maybe it does. As a child and teenager I recall some very bitter disappointments."

"Tell me about some of them," I said.

"Well, one big rejection occurred when I was seven. I wanted to go to a two-week camp—all my young friends were going—but my parents simply said no. They gave me no reasons at all. They just said no. On another occasion, I wanted to learn how to play a trumpet. But again, it was a no with no reason given as to why. When I was sixteen, I desperately wanted to date a boy in my class, but again it was no. It seems every time I asked for something I really wanted, I got a negative response. Now, I even harbor a little hatred for my parents."

"Hold it," I said. "Don't be angry with your parents. In all probability, they were doing what they thought was best for you."

I went on to point out that, as I see it, the two most important activities people perform in a free society are rearing children and voting, and most people receive little if any instruction on how to perform either function well.

I said to Becky, "Your parents probably did what they thought was best for you. Please try to understand that."

Becky smiled and commented, "You may be right. But what do I do now? I'm thirty and there is a lot out there I want. But I still have this horrible fear of rejection."

Then I observed, "Becky, until we reach adulthood, we are largely controlled by the actions of others—parents, teachers, and so on. We are captives of our fate, not captains of it."

Then I made four suggestions. "First, develop your own behavioral modification program. It is true that most people's adult behavior reflects their childhood experiences. But adults can, if they really work at it, change their attitudes."

I emphasized, "It does take work. Conquer the fear of rejection. As you learned in your youth, the worst thing that can happen when you ask is to hear no.

"Second," I suggested, "expect some rejection. Salespeople, for example, hear no far more than yes. Most requests of any kind are more likely to be turned down than granted. So accept some rejection. But," I added, "the more times you make a request, the greater are the odds that you will hear yes. A baseball player is a huge success if he can make one hit in every three times at bat. You'll be a huge success if one third of your requests are granted.

"Third, practice asking," I advised, "because the more you ask, the faster your fear of rejection will disappear. Do the thing you fear, and fear will disappear.

"Finally," I said, "make a list of the things you want most and then ask for them. Include in your list anything you feel would help you to enjoy life more."

Two years have passed since that forty-five-minute conversation in the coffee shop. Two weeks ago, I received a wonderful letter from Becky. Let me share it with you.

Dear Dr. Schwartz:

Hi! Do you remember our conversation in St. Louis about two years ago? You gave me some advice on asking. Well, I followed your plan and it worked. As you suggested, I made a list of the things I wanted most and then I asked for them. Here are the results:

1. I wanted to remarry my husband, whom I had divorced three years ago. I had asked three times before, but he had always refused because he was afraid it wouldn't work out. But I kept on asking and he finally agreed. We're very happy now.

2. I wanted to get our daughter some special medical service to correct a birth defect. I didn't tell you about her, but she is seven years old and was born with a hearing disability. It took five askings, but we finally got the treatment under terms we can afford. She's soon going to hear normally.

3. I wanted to finish my degree, but I simply couldn't afford the time to take a lot of courses that were required but didn't relate to my field. After asking five administrators at the university, I got them to waive most of the unrelated courses.

4. Finally, I wanted a higher paying, more enjoyable job. I asked nine prospective employers for a job and, you guessed it, I got the position I wanted.

Thanks for your help. Asking is making my life a lot better.

> Sincerely,
>
> Becky

## Practice Asking: How Can I Do Better?

One of the rules of organized society is that we all must report to and be held accountable to someone else. Even the President of the United States is accountable to the Congress and the millions of citizens it represents.

And our success in organized society depends on how well we perform. Doing what we do better is a key to advancement.

I met Walter F. after conducting a seminar that included a discussion of the technique of asking. Walter said to me, "David, I picked up some good ideas today, especially the one about rewarding people who sincerely want to improve their performance."

I thanked him and asked Walter what had been his experience in rewarding people who wanted to improve.

"Well," he said, "let me illustrate. As a management analyst in my company, one of my responsibilities is to review complaints from employees who feel they have been unfairly evaluated by their superiors. We have formal employee appraisals once every six months.

"About a year ago," Walter went on, "I had to review two complaints, one from a fellow named James and another from a woman named Mabel. Both had rated six-point-five on a ten-point scale. Ratings are important in our company, because a rating of eight-point-five or better qualifies the employee for a bonus and may lead to a promotion.

"James came into my office mad as he could be," Walter continued. "He began by saying, 'I got a six-point-five rating and I'm worth at least eight-point-five or nine.'

"Then he went on into a tirade about the unfairness of the appraisal system, the fact he'd been with us three years, that his boss, who is a female, is prejudiced, that other employees made his performance look bad, and so on. It was all I could do to calm him down to the point where he would not file some kind of legal action against the company.

"My next interview was with Mabel. What a difference," Walter explained. "Mabel came in and said to me, 'I need help. I'm very disappointed in my six-point-five rating. But I'm not here to argue about it. I realize the three people who made the evaluations are thoroughly experienced in this sort of thing, and I know they have nothing to gain personally by giving me a high or low rating. What I want to know is how can I improve? How can I do better?'

"When people ask these questions," Walter continued, "they almost always move up and they also enjoy work a lot more. Because Mabel was open, receptive to suggestion, and eager to improve, I was able to give her some concrete advice. I'm sure when the ratings are made again, she'll score much higher."

The message is clear. When we receive low evaluations, we feel resentful, angry. But turn this around. Ask for help. Never try to defend poor performance.

## Ask Only Experts for Specialized Knowledge

A common mistake many people make is to try to find the lowest-cost professional they can. But in practice, there is surprisingly little difference in fees charged by the best and the worst advice giver. So seek out the very best. Ask knowledgeable people. And when you interview the professional for the first time, make sure you ask about his or her credentials—education, experience, post-graduate training, and references. Someone who is truly professional will welcome the opportunity to tell you what he or she can do well and what he or she is not especially qualified to do. The true professional will be happy to recommend another specialist who can perform the service you need for the best possible care. I have visited the same dentist for twenty years, but when it came time to have my wisdom teeth removed, he told me, "I can do the work, but I know Dr. D. can do it better. Let me set up an appointment for you with him." That is the attitude of a true professional.

The point: Establish contact with professionals who (a) can service most of your health and investment needs, and (b) can refer you to in-depth specialists should the need arise.

## Ask for Forgiveness—Patch Up Friendships Fast

On occasion I've been criticized by colleagues and people close to me for wanting everyone to love me. Actually, I take this as a compliment, since I do want everyone I know to love—or at least respect—me. Even one enemy is more than you or I need.

But how do we eliminate enemies or at least keep them to as small a number as possible? An old country politician gave me the best answer I've ever heard. Let me share it with you.

My friend, now in his late seventies, told me, "In the past fifty years, I've bumped heads with an awful lot of people. In my county, people take opposite sides on just about everything—taxes, zoning, road construction, sewage disposal, school budgets, new industry—you name it. I have yet to see a hundred percent consensus in my fifty-two years of public service.

"When someone strongly disagrees with me, maybe even shouts at me at a public meeting, the very next day I either drive over to see him or phone him and sincerely ask him to forgive me if my plans or ideas offended him.

"In a minute or two, he's no longer mad at me, and I've either won him over to my way of thinking or we've taken the conflict out of the emotional area and put it into an objective perspective where we can discuss it logically.

"My habit works. I sort of pattern myself after Lyndon Johnson. Some folks didn't like him, but he was a master at dealing with people. One of the rules he lived by was, 'Sincerely attempt to heal every misunderstanding you have had or now have. Drain off your grievances.'"

Here are three excellent points for asking for forgiveness and gaining more.

1. Take the initiative. Don't wait for the other person in a conflict situation to apologize. You take the lead in getting things patched up.

2. Remember, asking for forgiveness is a sign of strength, not weakness. The let-him-apologize-to-me-because-he-is-at-fault attitude may be human nature. But human nature is often wrong. Extra-strong people ask for forgiveness.

3. Be absolutely sincere when you ask for forgiveness. Even a dog knows when you're lying, and people are smarter than dogs.

## Five Special Techniques for Asking

Let me repeat again the biblical maxim that is the basis for this chapter: "Ask, and it shall be given unto you. Seek, and ye shall find. Knock, and it shall be opened unto you." When applied properly, this powerful lesson works. Below are five suggestions to make it extra easy to use the "Power Proverb" in everyday situations:

*Technique #1: Expect some rejection. It will help you grow.* Becky S. learned to fear rejection because she had been denied so often what she truly wanted when she was a child. Be ready to accept these possibilities: (a) It may be beyond the power of the person you ask to give you what you want. For example, you may ask someone to buy something from you and they simply don't have the money. (b) You may ask for a promotion, but be denied it temporarily because you do, in fact, need more experience. But don't let this put a permanent stop on your dream. Learn more, wait a while, and ask again.

Learn to accept no. It's said that an athlete really isn't an athlete until he's been in a tough contest. And those of us in the field of persuasion—people who succeed by our ability to get other people to do things—aren't really veterans of the asking process until we've heard no a lot of times and learned to accept it.

*Technique #2: Reject unsolicited advice.* Believe it or not, most of the advice you will receive in your lifetime will be unsought, unsolicited by you. For example, when you join a new company, chances are that when you are there only a day or two, some old-timer (who may have started out as a mail boy thirty-three years ago and has now risen to chief mail clerk) will give you some solid advice. These are the folks who take you aside and tell you, "Now, if I were you, here's what I would do," or "If you always look like you're busy, they won't give you as much to do." But these advisors aren't you and they are generally very mediocre, so why listen?

The thrust of their recommendations center on "how to get by without being given extra work," or "why you should never disagree with the boss," or "how to make sure you never have to work overtime," or "how to avoid making the boss angry."

Unsolicited advice in work situations is almost always bad, because it generally comes from failures. Now, if you want to give up smoking, you won't ask a three-pack-a-day smoker how to do it. And if you want to rise in the organization, you shouldn't listen to someone who hasn't been promoted in twenty years to tell you how to move up the ladder.

Virtually all the good advice you will receive in your life will be the advice you ask for. Solicit advice from proven experts. They won't volunteer it, but they will give it readily when asked.

*Technique #3: Ask—never, never beg.* Asking and begging, though often confused, have different meanings. Asking means calling on someone for information, expressing a request or offering something in exchange for something else. Asking is positive and to be admired.

Begging, on the other hand, means seeking charity, bending and bowing. We associate beggars with poverty, misery, and denial. Begging is negative and is not admired.

In modern times, we have institutionalized begging through government aid programs. People have been taught that it's perfectly okay to get food for nothing or for a fraction of what it is worth.

Back in the deep depression of the 1930's, people had far more self-respect. They would knock on your door and ask for food in exchange for chopping some wood or performing some other chore. They were not beggars; they were traders, a perfectly honorable activity.

Practice asking, never beg. Examples of begging appeals that don't work are:

"I'm working my way through college. Won't you help out?" Most people will see right through this deception. Instead, keep concentrating on why it is to the buyer's self-interest to make the purchase. Again, appeal to the buyer's interest—don't beg.

Another example: "Professor, if you raise my grade by only one letter, I can get into graduate school." Here, the individual is asking the professor to do something that will likely violate his ethics. Instead of raising the grade, he may lower it!

Instead, say, "Professor, I goofed. What can I do to raise my grade by one letter so I can get into graduate school?"

Remember, begging reduces you. It lowers your self-esteem. And it rarely pays off.

I'm not a marriage counselor, but a lot of individuals who want to be reunited with their mates seek my advice nonetheless. Often they tell me, "I've begged him [or her] to take me back, but he [or she] says no."

In situations like these, I point out the stupidity of begging and suggest a different approach. I recommend asking the former partner for forgiveness, promising that you will try to modify your behavior and demonstrate your true love for the other person. Former or estranged marriage partners detest the begging approach. Ask, don't beg, if you want to put a relationship back together.

*Technique #4: Ask several times. But always in a different way.* There's an old saying that contains a lot of wisdom. "When someone says no, they really mean maybe. And when a person says maybe, they really mean yes."

Here's a suggestion that can make you a lot of money and bring you much satisfaction. Here's how it works. After you have made a proposition to someone and they have said no, wait a day or two and tell him or her that you forgot to discuss a couple of points that bear heavily on the situation.

Ask for another appointment. Chances are the person will give it to you. Then present your proposition in a new way, and again ask for the order.

A friend of mine who specialized in helping people set up businesses in their homes uses this technique with amazing success. He told me recently that at least one out of two couples who told him no when he presented the plan the first time, told him yes when he presented it the second time.

The point: Keep asking. If at first you don't succeed, ask, ask, and ask again.

Ask and Succeed! Remember:

- Successful people are askers. Asking will get you more love, money, and respect.
- Choose a mentor, a guide, a successful person who wants to help you—if you just ask.
- Asking someone for advice is the sincerest praise you can give him.
- Want a promotion? Then ask for it.
- Always ask people for help—never give orders.
- Phrase your questions to get a yes response.
- Asking questions is a sign of intelligence, not stupidity.
- If someone has wronged you, ask for corrective action.
- Ask, "How can I do better?" Don't try to defend mediocre performance.
- When you ask:
    a) Expect some rejection.
    b) Ignore unsolicited advice.
    c) Ask—never beg.
    d) Ask several times, but always in a different way.

**8**

# How to Win Influence Through Charisma and Commitment

Over the years, I've watched a lot of people with big goals come and go. People who achieve great goals have a number of attributes in common. If you observe successful people close up, you'll find two ingredients are always present: charisma and commitment. Let's discover why these qualities are essential to attaining more and how they can be developed.

## How to Develop Charisma and Stand Out Among People

Why do you immediately warm up to some people when you first meet them? At the other extreme, why do some people turn you off in only a few seconds? Much of the answer is found in a person's charisma or lack of it. Charisma originally meant a divinely conferred gift or power. Today charisma means a personal quality that gives a person influence, power, and authority over others. Like all great powers, charisma is intangible; it cannot be seen, weighed, measured. A billion dollars won't buy it. Charisma can only be acquired through careful spiritual development.

Jogging several miles a day, living on a nutritious diet, having cosmetic surgery to fix what is "wrong," taking vitamins, getting adequate rest, not smoking or drinking—all these may add to your health and make you feel better.

Excellent health and a great physical appearance are desirable goals. But feeling great and looking great do not produce charismatic power. The magnetic, attractive personality does not come from the outside; it comes from the inside, your spirit.

Let me tell you about Harry G. and relay his advice on developing charisma—the indispensible key to winning more influence over people and enjoying more rewards in the process.

Harry is the chief executive officer for one of America's largest companies. Two years ago, he invited me to speak to a banquet he holds for stockholders who attend the annual shareholders' meeting. The year that had just ended had been terrible. Profits were down, sales were off, and the outlook was pessimistic. But when my friend entered the hotel ballroom to give his annual state-of-the-company talk, he was greeted by an enthusiastic, spontaneous standing and prolonged ovation. And when he finished his talk—and it was strictly blood, sweat, and tears for the next year—he was again cheered, with even greater enthusiasm.

Later, Harry and I spent some time together to talk about a consulting assignment he wanted me to tackle. But before we got down to that, I said to Harry, "Your company had a terrible year. Yet the shareholders love you. You had everyone there eating out of your hand. I've been to shareholders' meetings where stockholders booed—even cursed—the senior corporate officer. How did you develop so much influence, so much charisma?"

Harry was quiet for a moment, and then he replied, "Oh, I acquired it—all of it. You see, twenty-five years ago, when I walked into a room, no one noticed me. When I raised a question at a meeting, people yawned. I was about as dull and uninteresting as anyone you could find. Then I made a decision," Harry went on, really enjoying sharing his secret. "I decided I would study charisma and learn how to acquire it.

"Now let me begin by explaining what charisma is not, and then I'll give you my ideas on how to develop it. Charisma does not relate to body build. I know charismatic people who are very thin and some who are plain fat. Some are short, some are tall. Nor are charismatic people necessarily attractive or beautiful in the Hollywood sense. And makeup, face-lifts—those sorts of things—don't help anyone acquire charisma.

"You see," Harry continued, "charisma is a spiritual quality, not something physical. It comes from the heart, the mind, the soul, not the body."

"But," I injected, "if charisma is spiritual, can it really be developed, or is it only a 'divinely conferred power'?"

"That is a good point," Harry responded. "Look at me. I'm five feet seven inches tall. Now there are no drugs, exercises, treatments, or anything any physician could have done to make me six feet tall. And even with the help of the best medical practitioners, how long I will live relates more to the longevity of my parents than to any other single factor. The physical side of me—and of you and of everyone else," Harry went on, "is mainly the result of heredity. But the spiritual part of me—my charisma—is under my control. In other words, I can't do a whole lot about my body, but I can do a great deal to shape my beliefs, attitudes, and viewpoints—the spiritual side of me that determines how much influence I have over other people."

"Well," I commented, "you've explained what charisma is not—it's not physical—and you've told me what charisma is—it's spiritual. But what formula do you apply to make your spirit project such magnetic charisma?"

"Before I share it with you," Harry continued, "let me emphasize even more vigorously that the physical part of a person does not manufacture charisma. President Roosevelt couldn't walk, yet he had that mysterious quality called charisma to an extraordinary degree. So does Max Cleland, the triple amputee who became head of the Veterans' Administration under President Carter. Many, many physically crippled people have far more charisma than perfect physical specimens. Perhaps that's because, being physically impaired, they devote more attention to enlarging their spiritual makeup and power than do physically strong folks.

"Now, since you really want to know," Harry went on, "here are five guidelines to use that will help to shape one's charisma.

"First is to be humble. As D. H. Lawrence once said, 'Failures are the most conceited of men.' You see, no one likes or admires the person who tries to show off, talks like he knows everything, or brags about himself.

"After I really started studying to learn why only a few folks stand out and most people make a negative impression or no impression at all, I discovered something startling," my friend went on. "I learned that charismatic people—individuals who just 'naturally' attract other people in all kinds of gatherings from strictly business to social—never try to attract attention to themselves. They resist that temptation we all have to prove how smart we are. A person with real charisma never, absolutely never, shows off."

Harry's comments about humility being a characteristic of charismatic people got me to thinking. Like you, I know a lot of egotists, but not one of them is a person I enjoy being with. People with real charisma attract it, they don't try to force it. A famous actor once told me, "If you want to be a celebrity, never act like one."

Then I said to Harry, "You said you have five guidelines for developing charisma. What are the others?"

"Number two," Harry continued, "is so simple, few people understand it—simply encourage other people to talk about themselves. Let them tell you about what interests them. Maybe their kids, jobs, hobbies, views on what's happening. People would rather talk about their goals, plans, achievements, than listen to you expound on why you're great. So, ask questions, listen, and before you know it, the other person will think you're a terrific conversationalist.

"Now, keep this in mind, too. When someone asks you for your opinion," Harry explained, "quickly turn the question away from you and put it back in his court by asking, 'How do you feel about that?' or 'What do you think?' A good rule is to answer a question by asking a question.

"Remember," Harry advised, "ask questions you know other people feel comfortable discussing, such as, 'What do you like most about your new home?' or 'What's the best thing that's happened to you since we last met?' You win two ways when you ask positive, directed questions and encourage other people to talk about themselves. First, you win a friend. And second, you may pick up information you can use later when you need it to influence the other person."

"What do you mean by the second point?" I asked.

"Well," Harry explained, "after only a few minutes of my kind of conversation with one of my managers whom I see just twice a year, I know a lot about that person. Even in casual talk, I can learn how he handles himself with his staff, whether he would accept a transfer, his goals, how high he wants to go, those sorts of things.

"Now keep this in mind when talking with other people; it's vitally important," Harry emphasized. "Give them your full attention even if the conversation is very brief as in a receiving line, or if it's one of those in-the-corner-of-the-room visits that goes on for several minutes. It really irks me," Harry explained, "when someone is talking with me and at the same time is looking all over the place trying to spot someone else. That's downright insulting. I'd rather have sixty seconds of undivided attention than sixty minutes of fractional attention. Give me all of your attention or none of it is my attitude.

"Let me make another point about using conversation to develop charisma," Harry went on. "Many people tell me they feel too self-conscious to concentrate on other people and their interests. My answer to that is simply this: The key to overcoming self-consciousness is to show so much interest in the other person that you forget about yourself. Keep asking questions and listening and self-consciousness disappears."

Time was running short, so Harry went on quickly, "Now guideline number three is obvious, but most people misinterpret how it affects their magnetic power. It's the way they dress."

"But you said charisma relates to spiritual forces, not physical factors," I interjected. "Isn't the way a person dresses physical?"

"Well," Harry responded, "clothing as such is certainly physical. But what you put on your body is a direct revelation of your spiritual qualities," he explained. "You can read the spiritual side of a person by how they dress as easily as a billboard.

"And my advice here is never dress up, never dress down, simply dress level."

I told Harry I had never heard the expression "dress

level," and I asked him what he meant.

Harry smiled and jokingly said, "Maybe I've added a new term to our language, but let me explain. We all know that most of the time—certainly in business—about ninety percent of your body is covered with clothes—suits, dresses, stockings, coats, hats, shoes. Most people I find who want to cultivate charisma 'dress up'—they wear something that is striking, different, unique—to make themselves stand out.

"Well, they may attract attention, but they don't project charisma," Harry went on. "You see, a truly charismatic person does not try to attract attention to her or his clothing. If you want to be charismatic, you attract attention to the spiritual side of you, your soul—not the uniform you have on."

I asked Harry to elaborate.

"Look at it this way. If the main thing people remember about you is the way you're dressed, you're not on the road toward charisma. Often, at parties, I overhear women make comments such as 'When you get a chance, look at Harriet. She looks dressed for Halloween,' or a man says, 'Old George looks like he's ready to lead a parade somewhere.'"

"In other words," I suggested, "if you want charismatic power, you want people to concentrate on you, not on what you've used to cover your body."

"Exactly. Let me prove my point. Please close your eyes."

"What?" I asked.

"Just close your eyes," Harry insisted. "Now, earlier you told me you thought I have a lot of charisma."

"That's correct," I commented, "you do."

"Okay. We've been talking privately now for about ten minutes. Describe in detail the suit I'm wearing. What color is it? Is it pin-striped? Solid or plaid? What about my shirt, the color and design of my tie? Tell me about my shoes. My glasses. How many rings am I wearing?"

As Harry kept rattling off his questions about his attire, I found myself only guessing at the correct answers. Here I had been talking to a friend about charisma and specifically the part dress played—and I had not really noticed what he was wearing!

Harry was a little proud of his experiment, for he had proved his point: Dress level—dress so level that people concentrate on you—not on the way you are appareled.

Then I asked Harry what he meant by "dressing down."

"Dressing down is not nearly as big a problem for people who want to gain influence as dressing up. But it can be a distraction. By that I mean women who let their slips show, men who have runover heels and dirty shoes; heavy women who wear pant suits—those are examples of dressing down," Harry explained. "If you want to project quiet influence and power, don't dress as if you've just been released after a five-year stretch and given a hundred dollars to spend."

"Any special dress rules for women?" I asked.

Harry replied, "Not really. The key dress code for women who want to project charisma is to wear conservative clothes that fit well. A lot of women," Harry observed, "dress so they will be envied by other women. That is stupid. A goal-oriented woman never does anything to make other women jealous of her or make men go bananas over her body. When they ask me, I advise women in our company to always buy clothes that will still be in style a decade from now. You see, real fashion stays in fashion.

"My fourth guideline for developing charisma or magnetic influence," Harry explained, "is to act alive, put, animation in everything you do. Most people act dead, and death repels people—it never attracts them. Notice how most people walk. They make it look like a struggle. Or how they talk in monotones, afraid to put life in their voices. They say, 'How are you?' as if they're being choked instead of 'How are you!' as if they're alive."

"And when most people smile, it looks as though the smile was formed by a funeral director, not like something that's spontaneous, fresh, and alive," Harry observed.

"Even in something as simple as shaking hands, most folks indicate 'I-am-dead-and-should-be-buried.' Charismatic people always have firm, solid handshakes—not the kind that makes you feel squeamish."

Harry continued, "The fifth rule for acquiring and projecting charisma is the willingness to take risks. Remember, most—almost all—people run scared most of the time. I've learned that when I take calculated risks, people respect me. Feeling afraid most of the time, people are drawn to other people who aren't afraid to try something new. I know, for example, when I strongly recommended that our company should acquire a new subsidiary, a lot of my key people were scared. But as I explained the plan to them, they developed even more admiration for me. Put very simply, when you've got the guts to suggest something different or innovative, you may not make everyone happy, but chances are you'll win respect.

"Finally," Harry concluded, "my last guideline for acquiring charisma is to pay personal attention to the personal problems of 'ordinary' people. You noticed tonight when I walked into the ballroom how the audience genuinely applauded me even though last year was a bad one? Well, much of their respect for me is a direct result of my respect for them.

"You see," Harry went on, "I don't duck phone calls from troubled stockholders—I handle them myself. And I personally dictate twenty to thirty letters a day. I let our shareholders know I am working for them, I'm doing my best, and I'm here to advance their financial interests. I know I'm often criticized by MBAs fresh out of business school for handling phone calls and letters myself instead of delegating those tasks. But executives who have been around me for five or ten years know why I keep personal contact with people.

"You see," Harry explained, "my real job is helping other people achieve their dreams. And I want the folks who make up our business to know I am here in the flesh and in the spirit, helping to make those dreams come true."

In a nutshell, to acquire charismatic power—influence over others—just:

1. Be humble—never be a show-off/know-it-all.
2. Encourage other people to talk about what interests them.
3. Dress level—never dress up or dress down.
4. Act alive, put animation in everything you do.
5. Be willing to take calculated risks.
6. Pay personal attention to the problems, questions, and interests of other people.

## Keep Commitments and Gain Spiritual Strength, More Support

Developing charisma and keeping commitments have one thing in common: Both are spiritual in nature. It's true, of course, that one can avoid legally, or by trickery of some kind, keeping almost any commitment—financial, marital, job, or what have you. But failure to keep a promise results in spiritual problems—lost respect and decreased chances for more of the good things and friends we want to attract.

No one on earth admires another person for breaking a commitment. That's a pretty strong statement. Let me explain why it is true.

## How Keeping Money Commitments and Good Jobs Go Together

A friend of mine, Elizabeth W., is vice-president of personnel for a large chain of supermarkets. One afternoon after a day-long meeting devoted to the selection of key personnel, we had an interesting conversation. I remarked to Elizabeth that, based on her presentation, she does a remarkable job of recruiting and selecting good management people. I asked her what she does differently from personnel directors in other companies.

Elizabeth replied, "I really can't say, because I don't know the specific standards other companies use in selecting their people. But I can say this: We look very closely at how an applicant keeps his or her financial commitments.

"People who beat bill collectors, don't pay their debts, and stay in financial hot water may think only their credit rating gets a bad mark, but they're wrong."

"What do you mean?" I asked.

"Simply this: A record of not keeping your financial promises hurts your chances of getting a job with us. You see, many companies like ours retain a firm to conduct investigations of people being considered for promotion or being hired from outside our company for top jobs.

"Believe me," Elizabeth continued, "an important

part of the investigation deals with the applicant's financial record. If we find that a person has avoided paying debts or has been in some kind of financial mess, we won't promote or hire him, period."

"You do that even though the person has the experience and background you want?" I observed.

"You bet we do," my friend explained. "Let me give you four reasons. First, next to your obligation to your family, we feel that an obligation to a creditor is the strongest commitment you can make. Failure to keep a money promise indicates bad character."

"But a lot of folks today, especially younger people, don't associate beating a money obligation with bad morality," I commented. "They reason, 'Oh, the bank has lots of money. If I don't repay my loan, so what?' or 'The store has millions of dollars. So I don't make my payment? What's so wrong about that? Besides, they set up a reserve for bad debts.'"

"I know," my friend agreed. "You're expressing the popular view. But these people overlook the fact that not keeping a financial promise is stealing. Everything costs more when people don't pay as agreed, because banks, stores, and other businesses must raise their prices to people who do pay to make up their losses from deadbeats.

"Second," Elizabeth went on, "if a person won't keep financial commitments, chances are he'll avoid other obligations, too, like meeting his job requirements or keeping promises to customers.

"Third," my friend went on, "people who don't have a sincere need to keep their pledges are likely to attract other people who also are delinquent in character as their employees. A department headed by one big rotten apple will soon be staffed with a bunch of little rotten apples. Like always attracts like.

"The fourth reason we don't want people in key jobs who can't handle their finances," Elizabeth concluded, "is risk. People who get into financial trouble are ten times as likely to embezzle, steal, or even commit arson as are people with no financial blemish on their record."

There's an important lesson here. Of all the items on your résumé, perhaps none is as important as being able to say, "I keep my financial commitments."

## How Francis Kept His Commitment and Got Rich

Two decades ago, Francis B. opened a small printing shop specializing in business cards and inexpensive leaflets. Today Francis is wealthy, has a fine family, owns an excellent printing company, is well respected in his industry, and, most importantly, has a sense of fulfillment. Francis has gone beyond living more to living at the maximum.

I spent a Saturday afternoon fishing with Francis, and I asked him to tell me the secret to his unusual success in every key dimension of life. Francis is very modest and slow to talk. But after a little insisting on my part, he opened up.

"Well," Francis began, "I grew up in an old-fashioned family. Every Sunday the whole family went to two hours' worth of church. Then we would come home, Mother would fix dinner, and my dad would give my sisters and me a ten- to twenty-minute translation demonstration."

"A translation demonstration? That's new to me. What was it?" I asked.

"Dad would simply try to explain what the preacher

had said, using lots of examples we could relate to. Stories about why it is wrong to steal or lie or not do one's share of the chores. Now, often in his translation demonstrations, Dad would stress the importance of keeping one's promises. He drove home the idea that there is something sacred about a promise. 'You've got to live up to what you say you'll do' is the way he liked to put it.

"When I left home, I decided to go to college, but my family had very little money to help me, so I got a job as an all-around handyman for a storefront printer. I did a little of everything, from cleaning up the place to running the small press to making deliveries.

"When I finished school—it took me six years going part time—I decided I'd open up my own small print shop. I had about two thousand dollars saved, and at that time it was enough to get me started. At first, it was really rough. I started my shop in a suburban location where I was completely unknown. But from the beginning, I remembered what my dad had told us about keeping our promises.

"And I put his wisdom into practice. I kept every promise I made to a customer. If the job didn't turn out exactly as promised, I would redo it at no charge." (Here Francis told me how he still follows that rule. Just a month ago, his company had printed half a million brochures for a customer, but the color didn't turn out quite right, so Francis had his people do the whole job over.)

"And I kept my promises on delivery dates, too, even if it meant no sleep for two or three days. I kept every commitment I made. In the process, I made money, and about three years after I began my business, I was able to buy out another printer with a larger shop and much more sophisticated equipment. Then the real test came."

"What was that?" I asked.

"Well, one weekend my business burned down—a total loss. The insurance covered only about half the loss, and I was already deep in debt."

"How did you overcome that? Did you declare bankruptcy?" I asked.

"No, I didn't. My lawyer, my CPA, and my close friends all told me to, but I said to them, 'My name is on those notes and I'm going to meet my obligations.'

"It wasn't easy, but I eventually paid off my creditors and got started again. From that time on, it's been hard work, but it's been easy hard work.

"You see," Francis went on, "without realizing it at the time, by keeping my commitments I won enormous respect from my creditors and suppliers. They honestly couldn't believe I was willing to pay off debts I could have walked away from.

"After that experience, I had no trouble getting started again. I had all the credit I needed. Business has increased between twenty-five and thirty-five percent each year for the past five years.

"So," Francis concluded, "to go back to the question you asked, 'Why did I succeed?' All I can say is, I learned to keep my commitments. If my dad had not driven that lesson home, chances are at best I'd be just another small printer trying only to get by."

## How Jim Profited When He Renewed His Commitment to Patricia

After a seminar in Portland recently, Jim R., one of the attendees, related a personal incident to me. His experience reinforces the duty we have to keep commitments and the rewards we enjoy when we do.

It seems Jim and Patricia had been married twenty-five years, reared two children, and enjoyed the good upper-middle-income life. But about three years ago, a real problem developed. Patricia, who did not work outside the home, began to drink heavily.

As Jim explained it, "Just about every evening when I'd come home, Patricia was nearly smashed. She got in the habit of drinking all afternoon, usually alone. As soon as I was in the house, she'd make the accusations every married man living with an alcoholic hears, such as, 'You're seeing another woman, and when I find her, I'll ruin both of you,' or 'Why did you spoil the kids and deprive me at the same time?' or 'Don't I deserve as much attention as you give to your work?'"

"That sounds pretty awful," I said, "but you don't look like a guy who has a bad home life. Usually, it shows."

"Oh, my home life is great now. Today you talked a lot about how we benefit when we keep commitments, and that ties in with what I want to tell you," Jim said.

"You see, I was really up against it. I was tempted to leave Patricia. Four or five hours a night of her abuse was getting to be more than I could take. But then a solution came to me."

"Tell me about it," I urged. "The problem you describe is common, but usually is very difficult to handle."

"Well, one afternoon on my way home, I decided for no reason at all to stop at a nursing home and visit old Reverend Zeke. Now Reverend Zeke had married Patricia and me, and had been in the home about six years. But, and I'm ashamed to say this—I'd only visited Zeke once during those years.

"Old Zeke was in bad physical shape, but his mind was as sharp as ever," Jim went on. "After a few minutes, he said to me, 'You're a very troubled man. Do you want to tell me what's bothering you?'

"I told him," Jim went on. "I didn't hold back anything. For a while, Zeke just sat in his chair, and then he said to me, 'Jim, when I married you and Patricia, you made a pretty serious commitment to each other. Do you remember?' I agreed that I did.

"Then Zeke said, 'It seems to me you're forgetting that business about in sickness and in health, for better or for worse.'

"Zeke then told me to try to meet my commitment intelligently. He gave me three bits of advice. First, he said, don't argue with Patricia about who is at fault for the difficulty you're having. Chances are you both are part of the problem, but don't look at it that way. Remember, she's a little sick right now. By all means, do not tell her she is wrong. Show all the love you can.'

"Second, Zeke told me to help Patricia find something to do. 'Now that the children are gone, she probably feels unneeded—that her contribution is over,' he said. Chances were if she had something constructive to do, the drinking problem would be solved—at least in part. Boredom coupled with guilt is one of the biggest causes of the booze problem.

"Third, Zeke told me in every conceivable way to keep my commitment to Patricia. 'Help her and let her know she is more important to you than anything else,' he urged me.

"Well, I did what old Reverend Zeke said, and at times, it wasn't easy."

"What happened?" I asked.

"Well," Jim replied, "Patricia's fine now. It took some time, but she and I are closer than ever. The turning point came when by every thought and everything I did,

I showed Patricia I was committed to her and I'd continue to stand by her.

"I encouraged her to help other people (she became a volunteer service worker in old Reverend Zeke's nursing home). Patricia also got involved in a United Way organization. Put briefly, she began to feel needed and started living outside herself. Her preoccupation with herself is gone now. And we're both a lot better off."

## Keeping Little Commitments Gets Big Results, Too

We've seen why it pays to keep commitments to your family, in the money department, and on the job. But keeping those little, seemingly insignificant promises pays, too.

Here are three rules to follow:

*1. Keep appointments and keep them on time.* Not showing up for a planned meeting or being late when visiting a customer, potential employer, professional person, your spouse, or a date says negative things about you. It says you're forgetful, you think the person you were to meet is unimportant, you're careless, and you're undependable. So, when you agree to meet someone, meet him, and be on time. If a real problem comes up, let the other person know as far ahead of time as you can.

*2. Keep those "little to you but big to them" promises.* Promise to take the kids to a ball game, take them. Promise to pick up something on your way home, pick it up; promise to do a favor, do it. Promises come in all sizes, but keep them regardless. No one will ever know how many children are hurt, spouses disappointed, and friends put down because a single "I'll do this or that for you" is forgotten or ignored.

3. *Keep a confidence confidential.* Everyone you know—yes, everyone—has some kind of secret information they feel they must share with someone. But chances are on occasion you've shared a confidence with someone only to learn in a few days that person did not keep your secret secret. Do two things: If someone tells you something they want kept confidential, stash the information in your mind and keep it there. Doing this helps you win—and keep—friends. You establish the fact that you can be trusted. Second, if you have information you want kept confidential, keep it to yourself. Do not share the information unless it is really important that you do, and then only with someone you trust totally and completely.

## Resist the Temptation to Squeal and Get Revenge

There's an old saying, "My country right or wrong, my country still." It ties in with getting ahead by developing charisma and keeping commitments.

"My country right or wrong, my country still" means that we stand by our nation in good times and in bad. It can also mean we protect the integrity of our family, regardless.

Now each of us belongs to a number of families. Our parents and brothers and sisters are the first family we think of. But the company we work for, our church, the school we attend, the clubs and societies we join—these, too, are families.

Our loyalty to other members of the larger families we belong to tells a lot about how successful we will be in our goal-seeking efforts. Let me explain.

Try to think of even one tattletale, squealer, or informer you truly admire. Chances are you can't. Squealers—those who reveal the truth, give the inside information, blow the whistle, deliver the inside scoop—are universally disliked, unadmired, even hated. News reporters, police officers, and personnel directors may listen to squealers, but they never respect them.

Judas was a disciple and a member of Jesus' most intimate family. Judas' claim to infamy was his betrayal that ultimately led to the crucifixion of Jesus. Thirty pieces of silver is the official reason for Judas' behavior. But it is likely that jealousy was an even more basic reason why Judas betrayed Jesus. Whatever the reason, Judas is despised because he did what no one admires, he turned the tables on Jesus. Judas, except for his evil deed, is forgotten. Meanwhile, Jesus and what he stands for are admired around the world.

As a child, you did not admire the kid who told the teacher about the bad things another youngster did. And as an adult, you don't praise someone who gets even by calling attention to the evil being done by someone in authority. Here are two examples:

## The Case of Ted R.

Ted R. did what most of us are sometimes tempted to do. He blew the whistle on the misbehavior of his boss. Ted worked for a university. His job was to market to businesses training programs created by university personnel. His immediate superior, Jay B., was head of the activity. Ted learned that Jay was quietly directing some of the lucrative training contracts to Jay's own consulting firm. When Ted had a thorough understanding of how

Jay operated, he confronted Jay and, in a nutshell, asked for a piece of the action.

But Jay refused, pretending there was nothing illegal or unethical about what he was doing. So Ted made Xerox copies of some sensitive correspondence and called the press. Soon the story of misapplication of university funds was on page one. In short order, Jay B. was fired, three professors who honestly didn't know what was going on were censured, and the university was embarrassed to the point that the legislature reduced its appropriation.

What happened to Ted R., the fellow who squealed? How was he rewarded? Ted received sixty days' pay and was told his position was discontinued. He dropped out of sight, unable to get another job with a university because, simply put, no one wants to recommend an informer.

What Ted R. did not know was that the university was aware of Jay B.'s illegal activities and was about to deal with the matter as a family affair and thereby avoid hurting innocent people and getting a bad press.

Most organizations do, in fact, treat squealers the way the university dealt with Ted R. Managers in most large companies learn from informers about other employees who steal, attempt to sabotage operations, or in some way undermine company activities. One personnel director explained her company's position this way: "We don't condone any activity that hurts the organization. When an employee brings some misbehavior to our attention, we check it out. Guilty employees are dealt with quickly. But in one way or another, the person who blew the whistle is dealt with, too—transfer, demotion, or dismissal.

"After all," she continued, "we have an ongoing audit of activities and most trouble situations come to our attention. Then we handle them as constructively as possible. Under no circumstances will we reward an informer with more money, better working conditions, or a promotion. Informing is simply a way to commit organizational suicide so far as management is concerned."

## The Case of Jennifer Y.

For more than two decades, Jennifer had been married to a congressman. During that time, they reared three children, the congressman attained great prestige and power, and Jennifer became widely admired. To avoid the hassle of rearing a family in Washington, Jennifer kept the house in their largely rural district and the congressman commuted on weekends.

Then a problem developed. A gossip columnist alleged that the congressman was involved with another woman. According to the columnist, the congressman was a devoted husband and great father, but only two or three weekends a month. When in Washington, he was engaged in a secret love affair. Now, in truth, the story was a fabrication. The reported romance was nothing more than a business relationship.

But hearing and reading about her husband's involvement aroused Jennifer. Most people are inclined to believe the worst, and Jennifer was not an exception. Her reaction was to get even, destroy the congressman's good name, and make him pay.

The divorce action that followed was about as messy as one can imagine. Jennifer had "proof" that the congressman had been on the take from numerous government suppliers, drank excessively, was a negligent father, took government-paid pleasure trips with the other woman (his administrative assistant), and that she had made enormous sacrifices while he was enjoying the good life.

Jennifer's closest friend advised her not to make the divorce nasty. After all, divorces are easy to get, the courts usually make fair property settlements, and even though the children were grown, they would still be hurt.

But Jennifer told her friend, "Look, I'm going to make him pay for what he's done to me. When I'm finished with him, he won't be reelected, his friends will know what kind of thief he really is, and the children will stop loving him."

Then Jennifer told her friend, "I want more than freedom—I want revenge!"

Well, Jennifer, the squealer, got her revenge. Her husband was not reelected, though he started a new career as a consultant and succeeded. The children were embarrassed about the family squabble made public, and Jennifer got far more money and property than was fair.

But look what Jennifer lost for believing the lies of the reporter and acting on them:

1. She lost all her close friends and their admiration.
2. The children no longer respected her and became spiritually closer to their father.
3. Later, the guilt of her actions became so intense, Jennifer suffered a nervous breakdown condition that restricts her activity.

Wouldn't it have made more sense for Jennifer to get the truth? And suppose the congressman had in fact been fooling around? Would it not have been wiser—if the relationship could not be repaired—to arrange a simple divorce rather than "get even"?

An attorney of many years' practice told me recently, "You know, I gave up handling divorce cases a decade ago for one reason: I simply could not stand to see a divorce action for what it so often is—the desire to avenge oneself for the imagined or real offenses of another."

Then my friend went on to comment, "If couples worked as hard at helping each other as they do hurting one another, this social problem would end."

The desire to get even, to inflict harm on someone who has hurt us, is as natural as the motivation to want food when we're hungry or water when we're thirsty. Long before little Joy reaches the age of reason, she hits a playmate because, "I let her play with my doll but she wouldn't let me play with her wagon."

As we grow up, revenge becomes more subtle. Teenager Jerry is offended because he failed an exam, tells his parents that the teacher has it "in for him." So the parents seek revenge by complaining to the principal or making an issue of it at the PTA. Henry, a young marine recruit, calls his dad to tell him how his drill instructor is abusing him. So Dad writes his congressman to ask for an investigation of the outrageous treatment.

John feels his department head has done him wrong (passed him over for a promotion, ignored his ideas at a conference, given him a petty assignment). So John lies awake at night thinking of ways to even the score by making the boss look bad (spread a rumor about the manager being in trouble with his boss, deliberately foul up an assignment that will embarrass the superior, who will be held responsible, put forth less effort).

There is no long-range value or satisfaction in devoting time and mental energy to getting revenge or settling the score. It is usually much more rewarding to give the same amount of energy and thought to building an organization and performing constructively.

The point: Don't be a squealer. Try to help people instead. Protect your "family"—don't hurt it.

Practice these guidelines to win through charisma and commitment:

- Remember charisma is strictly spiritual, not physical. It is your soul made visible.

- To acquire charismatic power:
    a) Be humble.
    b) Let other people talk about themselves.
    c) Dress so conservatively that people don't notice what you're wearing.
    d) Act alive in everything you do.
    e) Take calculated risks.
    d) Pay personal attention to what interests other people.
- Keep your monetary commitments. It proves you've got character.
- Keeping small promises is important. Always:
    a) Keep appointments on time.
    b) Fulfill your promises, however small.
    c) Keep confidences confidential.
- Don't be a tattler or squealer.
- Resist the temptation to get revenge, and reap the benefits of your self-control.

**9**

# How to Come Back to Life and Enjoy It More

Most people are dead. I don't mean they have stopped breathing and have been put underground. Their hearts still beat and their lungs still process air. But they are dead nevertheless. Take a minute and look up the word *death* in a full-sized dictionary. Here is part of what you will read: "Death is the end of life. . . . It's the state or being of no longer being alive—a cessation or absence of spiritual life."

Tomorrow, as you drive down freeways, ride buses, walk on the streets, visit offices, or fly on planes, you will be looking mainly at dead people—folks who are bored, spiritually exhausted, lacking goals. They have no reason for living and therefore they are dead because they experience a cessation or absence of spiritual life.

The living dead represent all ages, come from all occupations, live in big cities, small towns, and on farms. They have widely varying amounts of money, responsibility, and status.

Here's how you can identify the living dead.

*1. Boredom.* The living dead are weary of their friends, work, living conditions, and the way they spend their free time. They are extraordinarily tired of life.

*2. Guilt.* The living dead feel enormously guilty for what they did, did not, and are not doing. Guilt takes on many forms—neglect of children, parents, and friends. Cheating and other forms of wrongdoing, and wasting one's life, are other common expressions of guilt.

*3. Past-tense orientation.* An irresistible desire to look back instead of to look ahead characterizes the living dead. To them, the past, while not all that good, was better than the present or the promise of the future. The living dead simply will not accept change as part of nature's plan.

*4. Perverse gluttony.* Those who elect to join the living dead suffer from terrible mental nourishment. They devour all the terrible news about wars, rapes, murders, and robberies. The living dead crave bad news to reinforce their knowledge that the world is in terrible shape.

## Coming Back to Life Means Beating Boredom

Boredom is an easy-to-detect sign of the living dead. The people you know who are living tiresome, wearisome, monotonous, and dull lives are among the living dead. They have no reason to get up in the morning and suffer from advanced cases of boredom.

Look what boredom does to people.

- Boredom is a major cause of crime. The old saying, "Idleness is the devil's workshop" is true. Crime among bored, unemployed teenagers is many times higher than among young people who work. Boredom awakens a need to do something exciting—like robbing a store.
- Boredom makes the brain grow stale. Your brain,

like any part of your body, grows weak when not used. Boredom discourages the mental activity needed to build a better brain.

- Alcohol and other forms of drug abuse increase with boredom. There is a correlation, for example, between the rate of unemployment and alcohol consumption.
- A dull, boring life contributes to most domestic problems. A monotonous lifestyle invariably leads to quarrels, wars of words, and often, much worse. About the only excitement some couples find in life is fighting!
- Boredom stops learning. Dull, uninteresting education is the main reason hundreds of thousands of young people drop out of school.
- Boredom leads to poor employee performance, accidents, sickness, and even premature death!
- Boredom is a disease. And like all diseases, it is bad for us.

## Boredomitis Is Dangerous. Guard Against It.

One of the most important factors in determining the level of success we achieve is how we spend our time, and what we do between five P.M. and nine A.M. has a direct bearing on how we perform between nine A.M. and five P.M.

Boredom is a form of psychological malnutrition. And psychological malnutrition leads to living death. The way work is structured today, much of the time on the job is actually free time, and assuming we work thirty-five to forty hours per week, that leaves a lot of hours to spend as we choose.

Psychological malnutrition may well be the biggest influence separating people who are alive from those who've elected to die. People who suffer from psychological malnutrition saturate themselves with the worst possible food for their minds.

Keep in mind that the body is what the body is fed. Leave out vitamins, minerals, protein, and other essentials for a few weeks, and physicians will face a big challenge to return you to normalcy.

Keep in mind also that the mind is what the mind is fed. Avoid positive influences, true friends, good news, encouragement, and other essentials of positive living, and soon the world's best head doctor won't be able to help you return to life.

Consider for a moment a typical day in the life of George, a composite of millions of people, some of whom you know well.

1. George gets up twenty minutes late because he doesn't like his job (so his subconscious mind therefore programs him for more sleep than is needed). Besides, he goes to work only because he has to.

2. After too quick a shower, George makes some coffee and turns on the early news. The newscaster joyously talks about an explosion in a mine somewhere, terrorist activities in a country George has never heard of, and a projected decline in the Gross National Product.

3. Next, George drives to work on an overcrowded freeway. (A lot of other Georges got up late, too.) The radio news is even more interesting than the TV news, because it's mainly local. There are up-to-the-minute reports about two murders, three rapes, two traffic fatalities, and a fire out of control. Then there is time for a commercial about Good Times Beer, and after that the news continues. Local unemployment is up, relief payments are up, the mayor is defending a councilman who

is accused of cheating on a road contract.

4. George gets to his office building, but his usual parking space is already filled. (Probably one of those hotshots who's trying to get ahead.)

5. In his office, George is soon chewed out because his part of the project is behind.

6. Shortly, it's 10:15, recess time. George and his buddy have coffee and rolls. His buddy confirms that old Harry is on his way out, the rumor about Liz and Betty being lesbians is true, and Lillian is there for the asking.

7. Then, it's lunchtime. George goes to a sandwich shop across the street, comes back to his office, and reads another chapter in the book *How the Impending Crash Will Bankrupt You.*

8. The afternoon break is about the same as the morning break, except that George's buddy has some new information on how low the salary increase will be.

9. Eventually, it's five o'clock and George is happy for the first time all day, because he can go directly to the two-for-one happy hour.

10. After three two-for-ones, George is ready to pick up Sally. On the way to Sally's place, George hears that two players are charged with fixing a game, Hollywood's number-one star is getting a divorce, and a former President's wife is getting a face-lift.

11. Next, George and Sally eat dinner and play the game of "top it" to see who had the worst day. They end up quarreling about how to spend the next weekend.

12. At last, George is back home and turns on the late news to be updated on the peace conference that broke down, an attempted assassination of a leader in a country that he couldn't find on a map if he tried, and the bad weather that is headed this way. Next the news is over and the "Crime Show of the Week" is on.

13. Finally, exhausted, George goes to bed and thinks

that the only good thought he's had all day is: Thank God, tomorrow is Friday. Only one more day of slavery left this week.

Exaggerated? Not at all. The above description of the "good" life will be modified by age, marital status, type of employment, and other factors. But it represents close to an accurate description of the contemporary lifestyle. And reading between the lines, you see the psychological malnutrition that exists.

Now, read what follows very carefully:

The basic, all-important secret to more of the truly good life is to overcome the negative influences of your friends, co-workers, relatives, and others who impact on your dreams and desires.

Please read the above paragraph three times before you go on. Understanding it and acting upon it holds the key to wealth, freedom, security, and peace of mind.

Just in case you are a hurried reader, let me expand the secret to achievement this way:

The basic, all-important, overriding, critical, absolutely essential secret to more of the good life (health, money, power, fun, respect) is to overcome (conquer, defeat, destroy) the negative influence (you can't do it; it won't work; be content to be mediocre) of your friends, co-workers, relatives, and others who come in contact with you.

## How to Beat the Boredom by Sharing Each Other's Problems

A huge, billion-dollar-plus industry of marriage counselors, psychologists, advice columnists, psychiatrists, and others has evolved for one purpose: to save marriages. Indeed, helping people to live together happily and harmoniously is one of the greatest challenges of our time. In some parts of the nation, there are more divorces than marriages!

Why? Well, the usual reasons given for marriage problems are:(a) mental cruelty, (b) drinking by one spouse, (c) incompatibility (whatever that means), (d) physical abuse, (e) "cheating," (f) mistreatment of the children, and (g) lack of financial support.

Now there are still many couples who don't get along but nevertheless try to avoid the terrible climax of divorce. These couples may hate to admit failure in keeping the most important commitment a person makes. Or they want to avoid embarrassment (what will their friends say?). Or the children will be harmed. And, of course, some couples feel permanent separation is contrary to their religious upbringing.

Just about everyone agrees that marriage is the most complex form of human relationship. But why do so many marriages fail? And why do most of those that succeed (don't end in divorce) turn out to be far less than happy?

I believe the basic problem is boredom. And I believe the solution to the boredom problem is to find at least one common interest that binds the couple together, harnesses their joint energy, provides a reason for existence, and requires interdependency of action. Let me give you one example I've followed for the past two years.

Betsy and Robert, both in their mid-thirties, are an upper-middle-income family living in a fine home with their two young children. Betsy is an assistant principal in a high school and Robert is an orthodontist. They quarreled constantly—rarely verbally, but rather simply by not talking to each other (and silent quarreling is often the worst form).

One weekend when both Betsy and Robert were in a

reasonably rational mood, they decided to talk about their problem.

Robert began, "You know, Betsy, I think our basic problem is we're bored with each other. I know you have no interest in my dental work, and I sure have no interest in hearing you talk about problem teachers, students, and the troubles parents cause."

"I agree," Betsy replied, "and I can't stand your friends and what they talk about, nor do I believe you enjoy my friends."

"Well," Robert went on, "I believe there are two things we're both interested in, and maybe if we combined our interests, we could turn our marriage around."

"Okay," said Betsy, "what are they?"

"First," Robert noted, "even though together we're making a good income, we're still very much interested in making more money. Maybe that's because we both grew up so poor."

"I'm agreed there," Betsy conceded. "About the only satisfaction in our relationship for years besides the kids has been watching our investments increase in value."

"Now," Robert went on, "the other common interest we have is growing tropical plants. We both like it and we're both good at it. Why don't we start growing plants for sale and retail them on weekends at the local flea market? It could be a lot of fun, and we could make quite a bit of extra money."

Betsy immediately came back to life. For the first time in years, she and Robert were one again. Soon they opened their weekend booth at the flea market and began making extra money they didn't need but wanted just the same.

The point: Find and capitalize on what you and your mate have in common and you're on the right track toward "beating the boredom between us."

## Two Other Surefire Ways to Beat Boredom

As you read on, keep in mind that boredom is a psychological drug, it drains your energy, opens your mind to negative thoughts, and often is a direct cause of physical drug addiction, especially to alcohol. Here are two more fun ways to replace boredom with the real joy of living.

## Find a Part-time Job—For Your Own Psychological Therapy

Tens of millions of people should work part time, not because they have an economic need to work, but because they need the psychological therapy only work provides. Millions of women whose children are in school, millions more retired people, and still millions more teenage children from affluent families should work because work can be fun, provides interesting experiences, and helps beat boredom. Let me cite an example of how one woman I know rediscovered the joy of living.

Barbara A. told me why she was working. She and her husband were very well off financially, but she was working in a jewelry store two days a week.

"After the kids left home, I thought I'd die of boredom," she explained. "For years, I had played the role of cook, chauffeur, and counselor to our three growing children. But when all of them were gone, I found myself going bananas.

"Being alone all day began to get to me. I soon became aware that several of my friends who also were mothers of an empty nest were drinking excessively. I tried that for a while, but fortunately stopped. I could see myself headed for real problems.

"About all I had to do was watch the soaps. After a while, all those invented troubles and conflicts made me feel terrible. I tried playing cards with other women in the neighborhood, but I didn't enjoy playing cards and I disliked even more all the petty, gossipy small talk that is part of the game.

"Finally, I visited a psychologist. He made his analysis and told me, 'The best thing for you is a part-time job.' He was right. I enjoy being out of the house a couple days a week. And I enjoy the work, too."

I feel that work is the best therapy for anyone, regardless of their circumstances. You, I, all of us need work to keep us spiritually, mentally, and physically at our very best.

## Try School, It Can Be Fun

Another way to come back to life is to go to school. For generations, people went to college to prepare for a specific career. And traditionally, they were young. A couple of decades ago, a person age thirty or older was an oddity in a college class.

But that's changed. The average age of college students in many schools is thirty, and it is going up.

One reason is that older people—retired military personnel, people who want to change careers, and many other people—see the need to update their knowledge.

But another reason—and it's growing in popularity— is that people enroll in college classes for recreation, not for career advancement. One of the most interesting people I've ever met was Joseph T. He was trained in engineering, eventually started his own firm, and became wealthy by most people's standards. When he was sixty-four, he sold his company and decided to go back to college. And for thirteen consecutive years, he continued to go to school.

Joseph and I had numerous conversations over the years. He explained to me, "You know, going to school is really fun. I associate with people much younger than I. I hear young ideas, I listen to professors discussing new theories. All in all, I'm seeing life in a new dimension. Most of my friends have either died or are in senior-citizen homes. I'd be dead, too, if I had not put myself in a youth environment. Now I've learned what self-actualization is.

"Last quarter," my friend continued, "the professor paid me a real compliment."

"What was that?" I asked.

"Well, he told me that I was making a real contribution to the class because I had so many interesting and useful experiences to relate that neither he nor the text materials could describe. In his words, 'You add a special flavor to what I'm trying to do.'"

Most of us live within easy commuting distance from a college. Regardless of age, you may want to consider enrolling in some class that interests you. Education by itself is no guarantee of success, but it is an excellent way to come back and stay alive!

The point: To keep a youthful perspective, associate as much as you can with young people. It's good for them and it's good for you.


## Conquer Guilt: It's Another Way to Come Back to Life

Many of the living dead have passed away because they cannot deal successfully with mankind's worst enemy of all—guilt. For many people, guilt stands between spiritual life and spiritual death. Guilt is simply a morbid preoccupation with the moral correctness of what we do. When we do something we know is bad, we feel guilty. Then the guilt we feel interferes with the smooth functioning of our mental apparatus. The net result is decreased self-esteem, self-hate, personal hurts, self-reproach, and greatly decreased efficiency at work and in everything we do.

Guilt that is not overcome leads to psychological illness. Meanwhile, guilt that is overcome brings about new self-respect, achievement, and more of the good things life should be about.

Everyone suffers guilt, because each of us does things we feel are wrong. Psychologists have argued for generations whether right and wrong are learned or whether man inherently knows it is wrong to lie, cheat, steal, murder, connive, and commit other bad acts.

But whether right and wrong are taught to us or whether we inherently know the difference is not at issue here. What we do know is that unmanaged, uncorrected guilt works harm with our self-concept and our day-to-day performance.

Since we all experience guilt, and since we know it is a destructive influence, what can we do about it? Let me give examples of the way in which two people came to grips with guilt and are now living richer, fuller lives.

## Guilt Made Alice Stop Intimidating Customers and Earn More

Alice G. related to me her experience with selling by intimidation and why she quit.

"I got a straight commission job selling limited partnerships in oil-well drilling ventures," she explained. "The prospecting was done for me by the company. The people they selected for me to call on were modestly well off." (Alice later told me the company knew the sales tactics they used wouldn't work on wealthy people; people with means are thoroughly experienced in investing and can spot a questionable investment in two minutes.)

"The sales plan given to me," Alice went on, "was to explain the proposition quickly and then close the sale. When the prospect was reluctant to make the investment or wanted some time to think it over, my instructions were to make very firmly a comment like, 'My company assured me you could afford this excellent investment—it's only five thousand dollars—but apparently you can't. If you can't afford it, I'm just wasting my time,' or 'I was told you are a decisive person, but it's obvious you're not.'

"Now statements like these were calculated to take the prospect's mind off the question, 'Is it really a good investment?' and make the prospect say something like, 'What do you mean, I can't afford it? Why, I've got X dollars in liquid assets!'

"Then the next step was to close the sale, and after the intimidation procedure, it was usually easy.

"Well, in terms of commissions, I did okay. But I felt very bad about making those sales, because the company's ventures rarely succeeded in finding oil or gas. But what really turned me off was the tactics I was using. I was not only losing money for investors, I felt guilty about the way I was doing it," Alice admitted.

"What did you do then?" I asked.

Alice replied, "I joined another company, a very upfront outfit that required its salespeople to explain fully and clearly the risks involved and never try to intimidate a prospect into making an investment. The marketing manager made it clear that every year we have a new drilling program and we go back to the same prospects and investors we called on before. In other words, it paid to be up-front, because repeat sales were the lifeblood of our business."

"How are you doing with the new company?" I asked.

"I'm closing fewer sales," Alice responded, "but I'm making a lot more money. My straightforward approach causes a lot of prospects to buy several investment units instead of only one, which was what my intimidated buyers usually purchased. And more important than the extra money is the greater peace of mind I enjoy. Now, when I sign a contract, I don't feel guilty or dirty about it. I feel really proud. I've helped them and they've helped me."

Over the years, I've come to the conclusion that it's the cheaters, swindlers, and intimidators who give selling a bad name. Smart salespeople are intent on developing satisfied people who will become repeat customers. They know the wisdom contained in these lines:

"Fool me once, shame on you,
Fool me twice, shame on me."

## Margaret Had Already Paid the Price of Guilt

Some of the guilt people feel is very deep. But sometimes we pay a large price for it. And sometimes guilt, unless it is revealed only to a priest or another person who will assuredly keep it completely confidential, can hurt the lives of other people affected by one's revelation of what he or she did wrong. Let me explain.

About a year ago, a woman called me and asked to see me about a personal problem. Over the phone, I learned that the problem was of a marital nature. I then explained to her that I am not a marriage counselor, but she insisted on seeing me anyway.

Margaret T. arrived on schedule. She appeared to be about thirty-five, was attractive, and seemed very nervous. After a little chitchat, I said to her, "How can I help you?"

"Well," she said, "I'm happily married. We have two daughters and I have a part-time job that I enjoy very much. My husband is a lawyer and earns a lot of money. I work only for the fun of it. We have a fine home and we travel a lot."

I interrupted and said, laughing, "Sounds like you've found the good life. I don't see a problem in what you've said so far."

She replied, with a suggestion of a smile, "We do enjoy a good standard of living, but I can't put all of me into my life. Sometimes I hate myself so much I feel like taking a bottle of pills and ending it all."

"Hey," I said, "that's going to the extreme. Death will come soon enough without any help from you. Now why do you think you hate yourself so much?" I asked.

By now, Margaret was crying a little and she replied, "I guess it's because I feel guilty, awfully guilty, about an episode in my life. Something I have never told anyone."

"Why not try telling me?" I suggested. "Maybe it would help. Just telling another person about something one feels guilty about often helps."

Margaret, obviously not at ease, but coping as best she could, told me her painful incident. "I grew up in a small city in Michigan. After high school, I took two years of business at our community college. After that, I moved to Los Angeles and found a job in an insurance agency. Before long I became a friend of a girl named Jane. About a month after I met Jane, I learned she was a prostitute.

"That really shocked me, but I liked Jane and we continued to be friends. Soon Jane began to insist I get into the business with her. She promised money, excitement, short hours—all that sort of thing."

"Did you go into business with her?" I asked.

"Yes, much to my regret," Margaret replied. "I was bored at the time and I thought it might be exciting. For two years, that was my life. I made money, that's true, but I hated myself for what I was doing and it was completely against my upbringing. Finally, I came to my senses, said good-bye to Jane, moved to another part of Los Angeles, and went back to school to earn a four-year degree.

"While at school, I met Howard. We fell in love and got married. That was thirteen years ago. I never told Howard about my two-year experience as a prostitute, and I feel very guilty about not telling him. I was afraid—and I'm still afraid—that if he knew what I'd done, he'd leave me."

Now, she was sobbing. I suggested she relax and be glad the tears were coming. Tears, I explained, are excellent medicine for the soul.

After regaining her composure, Margaret asked, "What do I do to get rid of the guilt?"

I thought for a moment and replied, "Margaret, you have three options. First, you can live with it as best you can. Second, you can tell Howard about it and take the consequences. Third, you can talk to the Divine Power that I feel is in your conscience.

"Now, if you exercise option one, you can expect to stay troubled for the rest of your life. If you choose option two, Howard may not understand the reason for your confession, become angry, and at some point in time even tell your daughters about the sordid past of their mother—something that could wound their sensitive minds very much.

"I recommend option three. Look at the positive side. You did wrong, but you pulled out of it. That's character! That's willpower in action. Most prostitutes just go from bad to worse. You didn't. You went from bad to good. Remember also that many—maybe even a majority—of females fantasize about being a prostitute, and many—perhaps also a majority—of males contemplate a relationship with a prostitute.

"You simply acted out a fantasy. You know it was wrong. But you are healthy, alert, a good parent, a good wife, a valued employee. Keep this in mind, too. The past is past. The pleasant parts of the past should be relived. The negative parts never, after we have learned the lesson."

Three months later, Margaret phoned. "I have exercised option three so successfully I almost forgot to call and say thanks. That terrible experience is almost out of my mind. Finally, I feel I'm on the road to a full recovery."

## How to Overcome Boredom Through Careful Selection of Friends

The most important element in your psychological environment is other people. Other people—the folks you work with, relax with, visit, converse with—these people shape to a large extent the way you look at life, feel, your attitudes. Each of us is a product of our ties with other people. Now your interaction with your friends is a process I call brain modification. If you are not satisfied with the way your friends are modifying your brain, change your friends.

Most—in fact, probably all—our friends are friends by accident. We just happened to meet them through other friends or because we work with them or for some other accidental reason. How do we go about selecting people that will be better, and more refreshing, friends?

Here are questions to ask in selecting a friend.

First, *is the person future-oriented?*

Does the person spend most of his time talking about what has happened or what may happen? A friend of mine is very refreshing. She speaks almost exclusively about what she is going to do in her profession (she is a chiropractor) to make it more rewarding, how she is going to redecorate her home, the next vacation, education for her kids. She reflects on the past only to learn what not to do in the future. You're going to spend every minute of the rest of your life in the future. So why not put your head there? All the money and wisdom on earth cannot bring back one moment from the past.

So choose friends who look ahead, who have dreams, people who want to make life better. Avoid folks who delight in telling you how bad life is and has been. Stay away from people who think life is a prison and all there is to look forward to is more years in jail.

Second, *is the person share-oriented?*

Most of your "friends" want to get something from you, not give something or help you accomplish something. To improve your lot in life, select friends who want to help you, not because they expect something in return but because they sincerely want to help you. Sharing means exchanging ideas and teaching new ways of doing things.

Naturally, you will want to share your experiences with the person who shares with you. Remember, the greatest forward step in the ongoing friendship-building process is sharing. A good friend is always asking, "How can I help the other person? What can I do for him? How can I help her solve a problem?"

Meanwhile, a negative friend—the kind you must avoid—is asking, "How can I take advantage of Bill?" "What can he do for me?" "How can I exploit our relationship to my personal gain?"

Now a simple test for selecting a friend and for being a friend is to paraphrase the famous Kennedy statement this way: "Ask not what your friend can do for you, ask instead what you can do for your friend."

Third, *is the person ambitious?* A characteristic of a good friend is that he or she has a strong goal orientation. He wants to do something—move up in the organization, make more money, support some worthy cause, do more for his children—in short, get ahead. Associate with ambitious people and your ambitions will be strengthened. By the same token, become buddies with lazy, status-quo, the-world-is-awful-and-getting-worse people, and soon you'll develop the same outlook.

To beat boredom then, choose friends who look to the future, want to share with you, and who are ambitious—who aren't just cruising through life as freeloaders.

Fourth, *is the person a complainer?*

Find friends who see the good, not the bad, in life's situations. Avoid complainers. People who spend most of their time with you complaining about their bad health, the bad economy, the bad work environment, the lousy boss, how terrible their home situation is, and how they wish they could retire, poison your brain, sour your attitudes, and endanger your health.

If you're bored with your present friends, replace them. Many friends are simply old habits. Most of your friends are people you either work with or share a relationship with, such as customers and clients.

Join new groups, attend a church or synagogue, and participate in some of the special events, join community organizations. Seek out people with whom you have no business relationships whatsoever—people with different professional skills and interests. They won't expect dollars to result from the friendship, and you won't either. Do this and you'll soon be out of the friends-no-friends rut.

To escape the dead and feel alive, follow these pointers:

- Recognize that a cessation or absence of spiritual life is living death.
- Avoid the living dead—people who suffer from boredom and guilt are past-tense-oriented and are afflicted with perverse gluttony.
- Channel your willpower to overcoming bore-domitis. It is extremely dangerous to your mental health.
- Conquer the negative influences of the people who impact on your desires and dreams.
- Consider a part-time job—it's good therapy.
- Try school—it can be fun.
- See your guilt in perspective and enjoy life more.
- Ask four questions in choosing a friend:
    a) Is the person future-oriented?
    b) Does the person want to share?
    c) Is the individual ambitious?
    d) Does the person avoid complaining?

If the answer to each question is yes, you've found a friend and a cure for boredomitis.

# 10

# How to Profit from Persistent Patience

When our grandson, David James, was about three, he developed a special liking for grapes. He really loved grapes. So David's grandmother, Mary, and I decided it would be fun to plant a few grapevines. It was springtime. David spent a weekend with us. On Saturday morning, we bought the grapevines, dug some holes, and planted the grapevines. David went to bed early that evening because he was worn out from doing his part in helping dig the holes and carry the water. Early the next morning, David awakened me by shaking my shoulder and exclaiming, "Where are the grapes? I went outside and looked. We planted the vines, but there are no grapes."

I explained to young David that grapevines took at least three years to produce grapes and we would just have to be patient.

"How long is three years?" David asked. "Well," I said, "three more Christmases will have to come and go." David looked amazed and replied, "That's a long time."

A little put off at myself for not having explained to David that a grape crop is not produced overnight, I carried him to a food store and bought some grapes. I had failed to explain to young David the principle of persistent patience. So I tried to correct my oversight by explaining to David that any worthwhile project requires considerable time between planting and harvesting.

Think about patience for a moment:

It requires at least eighteen years from the time a couple decides to have a child until that "idea" is an adult reality; a generation or more of time is consumed after a forester plants trees before he can harvest them; most of our giant corporations were doing business for several decades before becoming strong, highly profitable enterprises; and it takes many years of patient, dedicated effort to become a successful musician, surgeon, engineer, teacher, or expert in any field.

Persistent patience is something we all need whether we are three or twenty times three. We need it because it helps us accomplish our goal of more!

## How the Now Society Impedes Your Success

We live in a now society. When we turn on the TV, radio, dial a number, turn the key in our car, we expect immediate results. We gripe about the slowness of mail, even though most letters are delivered within twenty-four to forty-eight hours after being mailed. In making investments, we want a big return in just a few weeks or months.

Getting the job done as quickly as possible without risking accidents or incurring unnecessary costs is an admirable quality. The American nature to be in a hurry to get things done is one reason why we enjoy such an exceptionally high material standard of living. But to maximize our personal success, we need to understand the part persistent patience plays. Let me explain why.

## Impatient, Passively Patient, and Persistently Patient People: How They Differ

The people you know can be divided into three categories: those who are impatient, those who are passively patient, and others who are persistently or actively patient.

Mr. Impatient wants immediate gratification. When he places an order in a restaurant, he wants his food immediately. He is intolerant with employees: "I want this project out now!" Mr. Impatient is angry at the slightest delay, blows his horn at the car in front that doesn't race away like a jackrabbit when the light turns green. Typically, Mr. Impatient is less concerned with quality than with quantity. "If there is some imperfection in the work, chances are the customer won't even notice," is his view. Mr. Impatient also gets in and out of different opportunities before really giving them a chance to develop. One fellow I know well, now about age fifty, exemplifies Mr. Impatient. Armed with well-above-average intelligence, a college degree, and good health, Jim W. is, nevertheless, a failure in the classic sense. He admitted to me recently that over the past thirty years he's tried his hand in more than twenty different enterprises, ranging from real-estate to securities, initiating selling franchises, land syndication, and operating a chain of dry-cleaning establishments.

Jim has also been impatient in marriage, trying it four times only to succumb each time to the promise of a better life with someone else. Now, in his middle years, and despite the fantastic money-making opportunities of the past three decades, Jim has a negative net worth—he owes more than he owns. He confided in me, "You may find this hard to believe, but I simply don't know how

I'm going to pay my back rent and avoid being evicted."

Sometimes the grass is greener on the other side. But often it is not. Your exceptionally impatient friends more often than not are dressed-up versions of the hobo of years ago—drifting with no clear destination in mind.

Mr. Passively Patient is a whatever-will-be-will-be person. He is content to wait without making a fuss over a delay or taking action to speed things up. His theory is that time will take care of everything. If we don't get it done today, we'll do it tomorrow. The status quo dominates Mr. Passively Patient's outlook on life. "Don't rock the boat," "don't try anything new until somebody else has proved it works," "let's keep that idea on the back burner until we're sure it will work," and "don't take any unnecessary risks" illustrate his attitude toward business and his personal affairs.

Passively patient types generally make a reasonably good living, are not a burden on others, and are respected (but not strongly admired) by their friends and associates. Generally, passively patient people become bored with life, make no waves, and look forward to their old age (perhaps because subconsciously they don't really get any excitement from life and harbor a wish to be dead).

Mr. Persistently Patient is a different breed from Mr. Impatient and Mr. Passively Patient. He reasons like this: "Everything takes time, but I'm going to do all I can to shorten the time required. I am going to promote actively what I'm doing so that my goal is accomplished correctly and with a minimum expenditure of time. Mr. Persistently Patient selects his goals carefully. He reasons, "I'm going to choose what I want to do carefully and then give it everything I've got." Persistently patient people know that substantial time and considerable effort are required to achieve anything worthwhile. They believe in philosophical concepts such as "let's make progress on purpose," "the journey to success is made one step at a time," "standing still is the same as going nowhere," and "if the goal is right, no price in terms of personal sacrifice is too high to pay."

Persistently patient people feel compelled to build not only for themselves but for the generations to follow.

Take a few minutes now to review how persistent patience has built the great civilization we enjoy today. Then we'll look at how persistent patience can pay off for people like you and me.

## Persistent, Aggressive Patience Opened the Window to Space

Consider the persistent patience Wernher von Braun used in developing rockets that paved the way for space exploration and satellite communications. In the 1920's, as a teenager, Von Braun dreamed of man someday exploring the moon. In those days, the idea of human beings venturing into space was pure fantasy. But that didn't stop Von Braun. In the 1930's, the Germans saw the potential of rockets as a weapon and Von Braun was put to work building rockets. Using missiles for war was not the use Von Braun had in mind for them, and in 1944 he was put in jail. Soon his talents were recognized as vital to the German war effort and he was released. He was told to put deadly rockets into space against England.

After World War II, Von Braun directed the team that put the first American satellite, Explorer I, into orbit. His team also launched the flight of our first astronaut, Alan

Shepard, in 1961. Von Braun played the largest role of any person in the first moon landing. No one else did so much to introduce the world to the space age. And he did it through enormous persistency. Failures of his experiments outnumbered successes by ten to one. But he knew his ultimate objective was worthy, that it was feasible, and so he persisted. His persistent patience will have an impact on mankind forever.

## It Took Persistent Patience to Give Us an Interstate System

Back in 1937, there were few automobiles by today's standards, roads were bad, and there was little interstate travel. Yet President Roosevelt was convinced that the United States should build a network of superhighways to serve the traffic needs that were sure to come. But it took years of persistent effort to get the road-building under way. Finally, after years of debate, the plan for an interstate highway system was put in operation in 1956. An almost unbelievably persistent struggle took place for two decades before a grand idea became an operational endeavor. Now, of course, we take the interstates for granted. The negative people fought the idea with all their might: We don't need an interstate system, we can't afford it, it won't be fair to all states and cities, money should be spent for more worthwhile (giveaway) programs, they said. But the persistence of Mr. Roosevelt and, especially, President Eisenhower gave us the finest system of roads in the world.

## Persistent Patience Helped Columbus Discover a New World

In 1479, Columbus made a voyage from Spain to the Gold Coast of Africa. This trip gave him an idea. Columbus reasoned that if one could sail so far south, one could also sail as far west and find land.

Columbus had neither ships nor money. But he did have that success quality of persistent patience. In 1485, he asked the Portuguese Crown for support. He was refused. Next, he tried the English leaders. Again, he was turned down. But Columbus's patience was persistent. So, in 1486, he appealed to the Spanish government. The Spanish leaders agreed to study the idea.

In 1491, after five years of bureaucratic inaction similar to what we often have today, the Spanish commission appointed to study Columbus's plan said, "No, it is not feasible."

But again, Columbus pressed on. Finally, in 1492, he convinced the Spanish leaders that his idea of sailing west had merit.

On his voyage of discovery, Columbus again practiced persistent patience. His sailors wanted to turn back, but Columbus, exercising great leadership, convinced them to keep going.

The result of the persistent patience of Columbus was the discovery of the New World.

## How Television Resulted from Try and Try Again

Everyone takes television for granted. All one needs to do is turn the set on and push buttons that may bring a hundred or more different programs before your eyes.

We think of television as some miraculous invention of the post-World War II age. But enormous effort and a lot of persistent experimentation preceded 1945, when there were only ten thousand TV sets. As early as 1884, a century ago, a German scientist named Nipkow invented a device that sent pictures a short distance. By 1922, an American inventor named Farnsworth made further progress. By 1929, a Russian-born American scientist named Zworykin demonstrated the first completely electronic practical television system. In 1936, NBC had installed TV receivers in 150 homes in New York City. Its first program was a cartoon of "Felix the Cat." When World War II ended in 1945, television took off.

But the point to keep in mind is that it took more than sixty years of persistent experimentation to make black and white television commonplace. And it took another twenty years to make color television a reliable product.

Progress in any activity, whether it be your own business, technology, medicine, or agriculture, takes a lot of the "let's keep trying, let's keep searching for a better way" philosophy.

The examples above are just a few samples of the great feats man has accomplished through conscientious, often tedious, but always exciting application of the principle of persistent patience. And the future promises even more and greater giant steps forward, because any good, regardless of its size and complexity, can be achieved when we make progress on purpose through persistent action.

Some day we will put colonies in space, build a tunnel to connect England and the Continent (Napoleon had the idea in 1803!); most diseases will be curable; life expectancy will be extended by decades, and worldwide peace will become a reality. But to achieve these grand goals people should believe they are needed and can be achieved, and second, they must develop persistently active plans to attain them.

Now let's look at how the principle of persistent patience performs miracles in the lives of individuals.

## How a Little More Patience Improved Tony's Performance 100 Percent

A common mistake many people make is emphasizing quantity instead of quality. Let me explain.

Tony W. was a student of mine about fifteen years ago. He was a good student, learned very fast, but was very impatient.

Tony had the make-it-in-a-hurry attitude. He lacked the persistent-patience philosophy.

Soon after finishing school, Tony became a management consultant. I didn't follow his career closely. He moved out of the region and our paths didn't cross. Quite by accident, I met him at a conference in Phoenix, Arizona, three years ago. After a brief reunion, Tony said to me, "Could you give me some advice?"

"Sure," I replied. "If you think I can be of help."

"Well," Tony began, "my fancy car, expensive apartment, and good clothes are only a front. The truth is, I'm not doing well. In fact, I'm barely getting by. You see, I specialize in developing and presenting training programs for first-level managers. But I can get only a few senior managers to buy my proposals. They often tell me, 'It's a good proposal, but it doesn't quite meet our need.'

"I've also written two books on management development, but both of them lost money for the publisher and they won't gamble with another," Tony added.

"Would you look over this proposal for a training program that was rejected? I put forty hours into it, and I thought it was a winner, but they turned it down."

I reviewed the proposal for a few minutes and then I said, "Tony, superficially it does look good, but is it your very best effort? You said you put forty hours into it. Suppose you had invested four more hours trying to make it even better?"

"Well," Tony replied, "I guess I could have improved it a little, but I couldn't afford any more time."

"Look, Tony," I said, "after forty hours' work, why not spend ten percent more time—that's only four hours—to make a good proposal great.

"Let me make a suggestion," I said. "Call the company and ask them to let you submit a revised proposal. If they go along, go back and spend four hours making your proposal better. Never give a prospective client less than your very best."

I explained to Tony that if he were just 10 percent more effective in the proposals he wrote, he would earn 100 percent more. I made a specific recommendation. When you think a proposal or an article is as good as you consider possible, then invest 10 percent as much time as you originally put into the project trying to make it better. "That works," I explained. "Let's assume you spent fifty hours preparing a proposal for a corporation. When you think it is as good as it can be, then spend five hours making it even better. You'll find many little ways to make improvements. To big thinkers, little things make a big difference."

Then I reminded Tony that Plato rewrote *The Republic* seven times. Half-jokingly, I reminded Tony, "If you had listened to that old lecture I gave on profit through persistent patience, you would be at the top of the consulting profession today."

I got a call from Tony last month. He told me about some of his recent successes. A very important client had doubled the work their firm's account required of him. Overall, he said, his business was up 100 percent.

I said, "I certainly am glad you're on the right track."

Tony replied by saying, "You know, I owe a lot to what you taught me about profit through persistent patience. I feel that I'm really on my way now."

A good rule is this: When you feel you have done your very best in any activity, whether it's remodeling a kitchen, writing an important letter, making a sales presentation, or repairing an engine, invest 10 percent more time to make sure it represents your very best efforts. Remember, a lot of abandoned oil wells have proved to be gushers just by drilling 10 percent deeper! Remember, too, that every great athlete spends far more time preparing for a big event than he does playing it.

The point: Develop the patience to perfect what you do.

## It's Not Where You Start, It's Your Persistence That Counts

Many highly successful people started at the bottom—I mean, at the lowest level.

Consider the case of Volga. I met Volga at a meeting of managers of apartment complexes a few months ago at Pointe Vedra, Florida. After my presentation, he asked if he could tell me about his recent experiences.

In our conversation, I soon learned that Volga had moved from Detroit to New Orleans. He explained that in Detroit he had been a plumber. He tried for years to set up his own business, but he just couldn't put together enough money.

"When I got to New Orleans three years ago, I had a wife, three kids, and one hundred twenty dollars," Volga explained. "The first day I visited eight plumbing companies, but none of them would hire me. They told me they had plenty of plumbers."

"What did you do?" I asked. "Without someone to give you a break, it must have been hard to get established."

"Well, the second day I was in New Orleans I rode a bus down a long, busy street. I made notes of all the fast-food places on that street that had 'Help Wanted' signs in the window," Volga went on. "At the end of the street, I got on another bus and rode back up the street. I applied at four food places but they all said no.

"Finally, the manager at the fifth store seemed interested. I told him, 'I am a hard worker and I'm honest.'

"He said to me, 'The pay is very low, only minimum wage.' But I explained to him the low pay was no problem. 'I will give you first-rate service,' I said.

"I tried very hard," Volga went on, "and in six weeks I was made night manager of the franchise. I found many ways to improve service to customers and increase efficiency. I did what you talked about today. I did more and I did better.

"Well, nine months later the owner of the franchise asked me to come to his office. I had met him only twice. He is a very busy man and owns thirty franchises like the one I manage.

"When I met the franchise owner, I soon learned he also was big in real estate," Volga continued. "After only a couple of minutes, he said, 'I want you to take a job as assistant manager of a hundred-unit apartment complex I own on the north side of town.'

"I was shocked. I told him I was a plumber by trade and knew nothing about managing an apartment complex," Volga said.

"He smiled and replied, 'I've seen what you can do in the food store. You've increased profits eighty-three percent. Basically, helping manage an apartment complex requires the same skills you demonstrated in managing the franchise—talent in helping people, motivation, planning, delegating. I know you can help keep the complex fully occupied, get the rent collected on time, and keep the place in a good state of repair.'

"Well, I took the job—and at three times the pay I had been getting as night manager of the fast-food place, plus a nice apartment for my wife and children.

"That was two years ago. I am now the senior manager. Soon I will have enough money to open my own business."

"What will it be?" I asked.

"A wholesale plumbing business," Volga replied.

Later that same day, flying back to Atlanta, I had a conversation with the manager of a government unemployment claims agency. He really unburdened himself. "Every week I review hundreds of claims for unemployment benefits. People come in and I'll ask them, 'What have you done to look for work?' The great majority will simply say, 'I haven't been recalled,' or 'nobody is hiring' or 'times are tough.' Then they ask, 'How many weeks do I have left?' The attitude of these people is that the world owes them a living. They think the government or the company is responsible for their hard times. It never occurs to many of them to go out there and scramble. The great majority of people out of work could find employment if they really persisted."

My seat companion was right.

As long as human needs go unmet, there is no reason for people being unemployed. There is work for everyone who is even reasonably physically and mentally competent.

Volga got back on his feet by accepting a job few people will take. And he proved persistent patience wins out. It's not where you start, it's where you're going that makes the difference.

## How Persistent Patience Is Making Alex A. a Fortune

Persistent patience works. But only if we have a plan to back it up. Let me explain.

A pension-plan consultant I know, Alex A., earns over three hundred thousand dollars a year. One day at lunch, I asked him why he earns far more than most people in his profession. After a moment's thought, he explained his success to me this way, "I have a five-step formula that works miracles for me, and I believe it will work for others."

I asked him to tell me about it. "Briefly," Alex went on, "here it is. First, I do a good job of prospecting. By that, I mean I prospect all the time. I take the pulse of local business news. I see who's being promoted. My eyes and ears are always on the outreach for new and developing companies. At meetings, conventions, on airplanes, even when vacationing, I prospect. After all, I can't sell to a nobody. I can only sell to a responsible human being. I'm especially on the outlook for young companies that I think may be interested in some kind of pension or profit-sharing plan—those are my specialties.

"The second step in my program is a telephone call to

the top person in the company. I quickly explain who I am, my firm, my qualifications, and the investments I specialize in. Then I ask for an appointment. Usually, I get the appointment, because I'm always up-front—I never try deception to get a chance to visit with a prospective client.

"Step Three is the personal visit—I call this my diagnostic interview. During the interview, I learn as much as I can about the prospect's investment objectives, temperament, responsibilities, and personal background. I say little about myself and my company. The kind of questions I ask prove to the prospect I know my business.

"Usually, when the interview is ended, there is no interest in a specific plan. But I have opened the door.

"Step Four in my program," Alex continued, "is to follow up the personal visit with a brief personal letter telling the prospect that I enjoyed meeting him or her, and that my staff and I are working on some specific recommendations. The personal note is vital. It conveys sincerity and makes the prospect feel special and important. In this age of word processing, it would be easy to send out a form letter. But that produces negative results. People are getting tired of simply being a name in a computer."

"What do you do after the personal note?" I asked. "What is Step Five?"

"Well, I follow up the letter with a phone call three or four days later. I again tell the prospect how much I enjoyed meeting him or her and I will do all I can to help him or her become a successful investor. Then I ask for another appointment.

"When I meet the prospect the second time, I come prepared with some specific recommendations. More often than not, no sale results, but I never act pushy. You see, I want to develop a long-term relationship.

"Successful selling is a lot like successful fishing. If you hurry things too much, the fish will get away. And if I appear too quick to draw up a contract, especially when tens of thousands of dollars are involved, the prospect will have second thoughts about doing business with me.

"But after the second visit, it's easy for me to discuss my plan with the prospect either in person or by phone. I keep in touch with the prospect until my objective is achieved. Sometimes it takes several years, but in time I close five out of six prospects I contact."

"I never heard of such a high closing ratio," I commented.

"Nor have I," Alex smiled.

As we finished our coffee, my friend told me, "I've got to leave and close a sale. For three years, I have been working with a prospect. This morning he called and told me he is interested in a pension plan I recommended. I thanked him and told him I would be by this afternoon at his convenience to finalize the details. This company has a very attractive income, and I'm sure after three years of working with him, my investment will pay off."

"I wager it will," I said, and we parted.

Persist, persist, and persist. But always according to a proven plan.

## Try Persistent Patience to Lose Weight

Have you ever been embarrassed when you should immediately recognize someone but don't? This happened to me last month on an airport shuttle bus. I climbed aboard, sat down, and immediately a man seated directly across from me—the only other person aboard—said, "Good morning. How are you doing? Haven't seen you in at least a year."

I looked at him and said, "I'm fine, thanks." It must have been obvious that I didn't recognize him, so he said, good-naturedly, "You don't recognize me, do you? I'm John P." Now I had known John for two decades, but this fellow looked like a stranger.

"I can understand why you didn't recognize me," John went on. "The last time you and I talked, I weighed three hundred sixty pounds. Now I'm down to one hundred eighty and holding. I guess you didn't know me because you are seeing only half of what you remembered."

"Well," I said, "you look great! But a hundred eighty pounds—that's half your old body weight. How did you do it?"

"Well, for years I tried every diet you have ever heard of," John explained. "Then I discovered one that was guaranteed to work. They promised me I'd lose three to five pounds a day."

"Apparently, it did the trick. You look in great shape," I commented.

"Like heck it did!" John exclaimed. "Two weeks after I started that famous diet, I ended up in the hospital. That crash diet got my metabolism completely out of order. I fainted three times in one day. I was in awful shape."

"But you must have done something right," I observed. "As you said, you did lose fifty percent of your body weight."

"What happened," John went on, "was very simple. My attending physician had several in-depth conversations with me. Now he is no diet expert. But he has a lot of common sense. He explained that it had taken me fifteen years to go from my normal weight of one hundred eighty pounds to my then current weight of three hundred sixty pounds.

"Then he said to me that only a medical charlatan would tell me I could lose one hundred eighty pounds in five weeks—that's over five pounds per day—without doing severe and permanent damage to my body. The doctor said the key is day-to-day persistency. He put me on a good, satisfying diet designed to take off only one pound a day. He assured me if I stuck to his common-sense diet, I'd be down to one hundred eighty pounds in six months, and it worked beautifully.

"It wasn't too big a price to pay," John went on. "After all, it took only six months to cure a problem it took fifteen years to create. And now I feel great.

"And you know, for every pound I lost, I gained ten pounds of self-respect."

As we parted inside the terminal, I thought to myself: Persistent patience pays off in every facet of life from making money to getting into top physical shape.

## And Persistent Patience Makes Money Increase Faster

One of the most interesting people I've gotten to know well over the years is Ben W., now eighty years old. Ben has a wonderful wife, several children, a bunch of grandchildren, and an expanding clan of great-grandchildren. He is also extraordinarily wealthy. Ben told me recently, "I really don't know how much I've got but I guess it's in excess of three hundred million dollars."

I worked with Ben in several capacities for more than twenty years. My most interesting encounter with him was helping him prepare his autobiography. He did not want his life's story prepared for the public to read. He just wanted to set down some basic guidelines for his existing and future descendants on how to make money and enjoy life.

I agreed to this assignment because I wanted to study Ben W. up close. I wanted to learn how a person from a modest background and only three semesters of college could accumulate oil wells, apartment projects, shopping centers, land, diamonds, gold, securities, and other forms of wealth.

Also, I wanted to learn why a man of such vast wealth lived in a modest home, drove a six-year-old car, and bought his suits off the rack in a department store.

One afternoon, as we were discussing his autobiography, Ben opened up by saying to me, "David, today I'm going to give you my philosophy about making money. Then you put it in my book [his autobiography] so my great-great grandchildren will know what I meant."

I promised him I would do my best, and so we began.

"I've always followed four principles in making money," Ben said. "The first one is don't let making money control you. I learned a long time ago that money destroys people if they worship it. Now, in my case, I've always given at least ten percent of my income to my church and other good purposes. And when I pass, much of my wealth will go to worthy causes.

"You see," Ben continued, "I get my thrills out of making money, not spending it. Some people like fooling with racehorses or gambling, but my sport is simply making money. I measure myself by my wealth accumulation."

"But don't you think this is a little narrow and selfish?" I asked.

"Not at all," Ben explained. "You see, when I make

money, I help other people do better, too. For one thing, I pay a lot of taxes. And that helps somebody. As I see it, taxes are just a cost of doing business. Now, let me give you some specific examples of how I help other people when I make money. Take the oil field I developed in Nebraska. I helped a group of investors who went into the project with me to make a lot of money. I made money for the drilling company and their workers. And I made money for the pipeline operators, the refiners, and the company that retails the product. And by taking the risk and finding oil, I helped in a small way to keep the price of energy from going even higher, but I'm not controlled by money. I control it instead."

"What's your second money-making principle?" I asked.

"In one word," Ben replied, "it's patience. I think impatience destroys the money-making dreams of more people than anything else. When I was young," Ben went on, "I had accumulated ten thousand dollars. To me, at that time, that was a lot of money. Then I met this sharp-looking, smooth-talking stockbroker who showed me how I could invest the ten thousand dollars with him and, using his clever formula, could increase that amount to a million dollars in only thirty months. Like a naive young fool, I went for his plan. Three months later after returning from a one-week vacation, I learned I didn't have a red cent in my account. My brilliant broker had lost it all. But the ten thousand dollars I lost proved to be the best investment I ever made. Three degrees each from Harvard, Yale, and Princeton could not have taught me as much about making and losing money," he laughed.

"What's your third money-making principle?" I asked.

"Hold on a minute," Ben replied. "I'm not quite

through describing the second principle. I can't emphasize patience enough. Once you learn how to use it, making money almost takes care of itself. Now I've been in the money-making business about sixty years. I was thirty before my net worth was a million. When I was forty, it was around five million. In the next ten years, it jumped to thirty million. By the time I was sixty, it was in the neighborhood of eighty million. Now, in the last twenty years, that eighty million has grown to around three hundred million."

Then Ben digressed a little and said to me, "You know, I just think it's awful that we don't teach kids in school what capital really means. Most of them think it's money to spend. But that's not what it means at all. Capital is money used to make more money.

"Another thing we don't teach young folks is how capital increases if you invest it with good sense," Ben continued. "Ten thousand dollars invested at twelve percent will compound to between three hundred thousand dollars and four hundred thousand dollars in only thirty years."

Ben paused for a minute and then said, "Let me give you my third principle for accumulating wealth: Never gamble in making an investment. Ever since I got burned in that ten-thousand-dollar deal I made way back there, I check out everything in advance. You know that shopping center I built? Well, I had three independent studies made before I went ahead. I wanted to be sure it was the right location. I do the same thing before I go into an oil-drilling venture. I hire independent geologists—the best I can find—to study the property to find out if they think there is oil or gas to be found in profitable quantities. So never gamble. Check out every investment very carefully. It's only a rough guess, but I estimate I reject at least nineteen out of twenty deals that come to me.

"Now let me give you my fourth principle, and it's an emotional one. Never take advantage of people you invite to invest with you. Regardless of how carefully I check things out, once in a while an investment doesn't pay off. I remember a situation that happened to me about twenty years ago. I had come across what I thought was a surefire real-estate opportunity. A medium-sized city was going to build a new airport. My real-estate experts told me they were ninety-nine percent certain where it would be located. So I put together a syndicate to buy some nearby real estate that would prove a good site for a motel, restaurant, and a few other facilities that airports need. I was so sure it would pan out that I encouraged my secretary and her husband to take a small part of the investment. Having confidence in me, they invested fifteen thousand dollars, just about everything they had saved.

"Well," Ben went on, "the city council decided on another site on the other side of the city. Our investment proved to be a real disaster. My conscience really hurt because I had involved my secretary and her husband in the deal. They simply didn't have the risk capital. When I learned that our investment was a severe loss, I wrote my secretary a check for the full amount of their investment. Never again did I invite anyone to participate in a venture if losing would really hurt them."

In a nutshell, then, Ben's money-making formula boils down to four points:

1. Enjoy making money, but don't let making it control you.
2. Exercise patience and more patience.
3. Never gamble in making an investment. Research before you invest.

4. Make sure people who can't afford the risk don't get hurt.

Not many of us have aspirations to accumulate three hundred million dollars. But Ben's principles apply regardless of what your goal is. The basic key again is persistent patience.

## Protect Your Reputation: You Can Lose It Overnight

People who strive for success want the joy and satisfaction that comes from earning a good reputation. To many achievers, being held in high esteem, considered worthy and meritorious, and possessing a good name is the greatest reward of living a successful life. After all, one cannot buy a good reputation. It must be earned.

And in most cases it takes leaders in all fields—athletics, business, politics, acting, writing, education—many long, often frustrating years of hard, patient work and considerable sacrifice to make it to the top. It is never easy to become universally admired or universally respected overnight.

As a boy at a county fair, I remember seeing a tragic sight. A well-known performer climbed a two-hundred-foot greased pole. It was quite a feat. For ten minutes, hundreds of people watched this man climb the unbelievably slick pole until he reached the top. Then something went wrong and in less than three seconds his body lay crumpled and spattered on the ground below. It was a terrible sight. But the point is that what took ten minutes to achieve ended in death in seconds.

We can fall far faster than we can rise.

The persistent patience we apply to achieve the success we desire can be wasted if we do not guard carefully and preciously the reputation we create.

After serving eight years as Vice-President, Richard Nixon was defeated for the presidency by John Kennedy. But this didn't stop Nixon. In 1964, when many Republicans refused to support Senator Goldwater for the nation's highest office, Richard Nixon supported him. And in 1966, when the Republican party was in disarray, Nixon stumped the nation helping Republican congressional candidates win seats in Congress.

Then the year was 1968 and time for another presidential election. Nixon, because he had stood by his party and had worked so hard to help rebuild it, was the obvious choice to run again for the nation's top job. This time he won.

In 1972, he ran for a second term. His reelection was virtually assured because his record for the previous four years on balance was good. He won the presidency by an enormous majority.

Then came the gradual exposure of the truth about Watergate, probably the most widely publicized political scandal in history. Because of Nixon's alleged involvement, he was left with only two alternatives: resign or be impeached.

Nixon had given more than twenty-five years of his life and had achieved enormous prestige and much confidence here and abroad only to have his reputation virtually destroyed in only a few months. Twenty-five years of persistent patience to build it, six months to destroy it.

Headlines such as these illustrate how people who worked hard for years to move up are brought down in a few weeks or months:

"Judge Found Guilty of Accepting Bribe to Dismiss Case"

"Parole Officer Lies to Set Convict Free"

"Senator Found Guilty in Abscam Investigation"

"Football Coach Fired for Violating Eligibility Rules"

"Senator Redirects Freeway to Raise Value of His Land"

"Welfare Director Pockets Twenty Thousand Dollars in Fraudulent Claims"

The people who are caught violating the rules of society make two huge errors. First, they damage—often destroy—the reputations they worked hard to create. And second, they end up making far less money than if they had gone to considerable trouble to be scrupulously honest in all matters.

Here are three suggestions for reputation safekeeping that work.

*1. Your reputation is your most important asset. Guard it.* It takes a lot of time and effort to build a good reputation. But once a reputation for creativity, hard work, and success is lost, it is almost impossible to rebuild. If you stumble, news of your problem travels very fast. Some will take great joy in saying, "He got just exactly what he deserved."

*2. You are an example-setter. Be sure your example is worth copying.* Whether you are prominent locally, regionally, or nationally, your views, attitudes, and habits are being imitated by others. The question each of us must ask is, "Is my example worth emulating?" One reason for the out-of-control use of hard and soft drugs is their use by prominent athletes, actors, and performers. One talent agent told me that every time a story appears about a featured personality using drugs, at least one thousand young people decide to experiment. And when a county councilman gets involved in a shady deal with a local contractor, dozens of other people try to make similar deals. The point is simple: Set good examples and help build better companies, communities, and a better nation. At the same time, protect your hard-earned reputation.

*3. Honesty still pays handsomely.* There is an enormous amount of money to be made in perfectly legitimate ways. If the schemers and connivers would spend half as much time developing ways to make money honestly instead of in some crooked and often illegal way, they would end up with far more. It's not stupid to be honest—it's the way of wisdom.

## How to Use Persistent Patience in Everyday Little Situations

It is not easy for most of us to relate to space travel, television, great voyages of exploration, medical breakthroughs, and other impossible events. But what about the little things in life that may be of no interest to mankind in general, but for us as individuals have enormous significance? Here again, persistent patience will win for us. If (a) the objective or goal is worthwhile, (b) you have the qualities to achieve it, and (c) you are sufficiently persistent, you will win.

Consider these examples:

## How John Won the Battle over Booze

John W., a middle manager in a chemical company, had been a steady and large consumer of alcohol for more than a decade. As his problem grew worse, his two children, while still loving him, came to disrespect him. And his wife only tolerated him. At home, he was consistently under the influence. And since it takes hours to become sober, he was usually partly drunk on the job.

John's superior had several outspoken conversations with him, telling him that alcohol was interfering with his performance, that he was doing continual damage to every cell in his body, not excluding his brain, and that he'd been passed over for promotions twice because of his problem. The superior even offered to send him—at full pay—to a rehabilitation center for treatment. But John wouldn't accept the offer.

"You make it sound as if I were an alcoholic," he told his boss. "But I'm not." That is usually what most alcoholics say when directly confronted with their problem.

Finally, one evening John's wife and the two teenage children had a direct confrontation with him. They assured John that they loved him, but said that they no longer could tolerate his alcoholism and they were going to leave him if he did not quit drinking.

The prospect of being left alone and giving up the people he loved hit John pretty hard. He made a decision on the spot never again to consume even a teaspoon of alcohol. He used the success reasoning: The goal is worthwhile. It means keeping my family and my health; I do have the willpower, and I will give it the maximum persistent effort.

Later, John told me how his decision had worked out. "For the first two weeks, living without alcohol was what I imagine living in hell would be. I slept very little, and when I did, I had awful dreams. But surprisingly, each day I began to feel stronger. I was winning day-by-day the toughest battle I had ever fought. Now, it has been three years since I made that hard, firm, total commitment to quit. And I honestly don't miss the booze at all. And because of my work, I'm around people all the time who drink. I attend a lot of business lunches, attitude-adjustment parties, and similar events where the two or more martinis or scotches are the rule, but I just mingle around sipping plain ice water or orange juice feeling sorry for my friends."

There is simply no substitute for total persistency in the pursuit of a goal!

## How Mary Conquered Her Fear of Speaking Up

A lot of us grow up feeling timid, shy, and inferior when around peers and our superiors. I had known Mary J. for a number of years. One day she confessed to me that she belonged to the "never speak up" club. Mary was intelligent, knowledgeable, and had a lot to offer. But in her words, "Every time I'm with more than three or four people, I'm afraid to express myself. I know if I say anything, my voice will tremble and I'll end up appearing foolish."

I assured Mary that her fear is as common as crabgrass, but it can be cured.

"How?" she asked. "I have a feeling that if I could speak up, I'd stand a better chance for advancement."

"You're certainly right there," I agreed. "Here are two recommendations. First, decide right now that at your next meeting you will speak up twice. The first time you speak, ask a question about the matter being discussed. Then, a little later, speak up again offering a suggestion about a policy or a problem before the group. Take these two steps persistently and you will overcome your fear in no time."

"But," Mary replied, "I don't understand your sequence of first asking a question about something and then coming up with a possible solution to a problem."

"Here's the logic," I replied, "when you ask a ques-

tion, you immediately prove you are not a know-it-all—
that you want pertinent information about what's being
discussed. Then, later, when you propose a possible solution, you're showing the group you can, by listening
and digesting various opinions, come up with possible
solutions."

Mary followed the suggestions. She told me later that
her fears of speaking up have been largely overcome because she persists in (a) asking questions, and (b) suggesting solutions.

If you are timid about speaking up in group situations,
try this approach. It works!

## How to Avoid Petty Quarrels with Your Mate

Over the years, I've talked with many individuals and
couples about problems with their mates. And I've read
a large sample of articles and books dealing with domestic problems.

Even in this enlightened age when informed people
should know better, the two problems identified most
frequently as the causes of domestic strife, divorce, separation and quarrels are (a) sex, and (b) money.

But except in extreme, rare situations, is bad sex (too
much, too little, technique, those sorts of things) or
money (its lack, which partner earned the most, who
spends it, and for what, etc.) the real cause of domestic
problems?

The essential difficulty has to do with the degree of
patience each partner exhibits toward the other. Here
are examples of one of the problems that is never mentioned in divorce:

Bill doesn't like to see Brenda with her hair in curlers, is unhappy with her mannerisms, is put off because she insists on talking while he watches "Monday Night Football," and complains about not feeling good.

And Brenda is ticked off with Bill because he leaves the bathroom in a mess, brings work home one or two nights a week, snores, and isn't overjoyed at spending a lot of time with her friends.

So they quarrel. And if they quarrel badly enough, they go in different directions.

As Brenda explained to me, "One evening we were both in a good mood and decided to discuss how we could resolve our conflicts and enjoy the happiness all couples are entitled to.

"We concluded that our problem was not a lack of love for each other. Rather, the difficulty centered on small, petty, unimportant habits and attitudes. So we reached this agreement.

"First, before we were critical of each other for any reason, we would say nothing. We would exercise patience. We would simply overlook what one of us did that disappointed the other. Love is too important to endanger it by cutting the other person down over some trivial happening.

"Second, when either of us did something we strongly admired, we'd give the other person a really big compliment. Because we both love to be praised, pretty soon our behaviors became more acceptable to each other. When Bill told me how nice my hair looked, I stopped wearing curlers when he was around. And when I stopped nagging him about his devotion to football on television, he was pleased.

"The net result of being more patient with each other has produced a world of difference. In doing so, we put love first and negativism a distant second, and indeed we profit thereby."

Persistent patience pays. Practice it. Remember:

- All great achievements require time.
- Impatient people rarely accomplish anything.
- Passively patient folks make no waves and make less money than they could.
- Persistently patient people always win because they don't give up.
- All great inventions and developments take decades to perfect.
- Where you start is unimportant. Where you're headed means everything.
- Persistent patience in investing pays off when you:
  - a) Enjoy making money but don't let it control you.
  - b) Practice patience and more patience.
  - c) Never gamble.
  - d) Make sure people who can't afford the risk don't get hurt.
- Protect your reputation. You can lose it overnight.
- Practice persistent patience at work, in the home, and on the job.

# 11

## Make a New Beginning

Because down deep we are honest, most of us must face this conclusion: If we keep our present it-can't-be-achieved attitudes toward success, continue to associate with negative people, make no positive adjustments in our attitudes, and set our sights on mediocre goals, then we are guaranteed a dull, uneventful, boring, and unrewarding future.

A losing philosophy always produces losers. That is a law.

But if we elect to make positive adjustments in our attitudes, discover what is right, not wrong with life's situations, make friends with people who are moving up, and set big goals for ourselves, then we are assured a large measure of happiness, joy, money, and influence.

A winning philosophy always produces winners. That, too, is a law.

Many references are made in the Bible to concepts such as, "Think like a child"; "be childlike to discover wisdom"; "only a child has perfect understanding"; and "a child will lead them." The message that comes through is this: To rebuild one's life—to think with clarity about the future one must become mentally a child again and start over.

Psychoanalysts use this twofold approach to help people gain a new focus: First, they help one regress to one's childhood and review how one's thought processes were shaped, and second, based on the clear thinking that comes from being a child again, restructure one's thinking, viewpoints, and attitudes toward positive objectives.

To understand the why and how of making a new beginning, view people as falling into one of two categories—losers and winners. Then contrast the way each group views the future.

## Losers See an Awful, Terrible, Horrible Future

Let's put the philosophy of the losers in closer focus. Imagine for a moment a couple we'll call "Mr. and Mrs. Settle For Less" announcing the birth of a child. Here is how the announcement reads:

Birth Announcement

Mr. and Mrs. Settle For Less
Announce the Birth of "Suffer Forever"

Mr. and Mrs. Settle For Less announce with disappointment the birth of Suffer Forever. Mr. and Mrs. Less were reluctant to give birth to Suffer Forever because experts predict mass starvation, all-out nuclear war, new diseases that will reach epidemic proportions, and a worldwide economic depression that will end law and order for centuries.

Even before civilization is destroyed, Mr. and Mrs. Settle For Less are sure Suffer Forever will be molested by street gangs, and led astray by evil-minded peers.

At best, Mr. and Mrs. Settle For Less see few jobs for young people, a Communist takeover, no Social Security, and a military dictatorship. Mr. Less feels the only sure business success of the future will be a franchised system of suicide havens, where people can end their miserable lives affordably and efficiently.

Because of the impending national-global disaster, Mr. and Mrs. Less have joined these organizations to help delay the certain disaster: "Hoard canned food now!," "Tax the churches to pay for abortions," and "Legalize cocaine to minimize suffering during the coming terrible times."

Does the announcement sound far-fetched? It isn't really. It reflects a sour, bitter, frightened attitude shared by millions of people who knowingly or unknowingly have elected to sign up with the "we're defeated" club.

## Winners See a Golden Age for Themselves Now; for Everyone in the Future

Contrast for a moment the views of the losers, Mr. and Mrs. Settle For Less, with the philosophy of the winners, Mr. and Mrs. Enjoy Even More. Mr. and Mrs. More are also making a birth announcement, but with thanks and optimism.

Birth Announcement

Mr. and Mrs. Enjoy Even More
Announce the Birth of
"Great Times"

Mr. and Mrs. Enjoy Even More are exceptionally happy to announce the birth of Great Times. The birth occurs on the threshold of the Golden Age. Good food is plentiful; the dreaded diseases that prematurely killed Great Times's ancestors—diphtheria, tuberculosis, polio, and many others have disappeared; new discoveries promise a longer life span; great adventures in space promise unbelievable benefits to Greater Times and all mankind.

Great Times has more choices than anyone has experienced before; twice as many careers to choose from than were available only twenty-five years ago; unlimited travel and mobility; a wide selection of lifestyles.

It is true that Great Times did inherit a proportionate share of the national debt—about six thousand dollars of it. But Great Times has also inherited more than a hundred thousand dollars of the nation's wealth in the form of interstates, dams, harbors, schools, universities, public lands (640 million acres!) and many other assets made possible by the sacrifices of previous generations.

And Great Times's freedom is guaranteed by the most liberal and best defended constitution on earth.

Truly, those of us who do see the forest know the Golden Age is at hand. Whether we enjoy it or not is strictly a personal, individual decision.

## Go Backward, Then Forward, and Profit from a New Beginning

A new beginning can be the most exciting, rewarding, and challenging activity you have experienced. Give it a try: Just:

1. Go backward in time to the point that simple wisdom is your guide, then:
2. Restructure your life around the goals you want.

Use the rebirth announcement of Mr. Start Over Right as a guide.

Special Announcement

Mr. Born To Fail Announces
His Rebirth As
"Start Over Right"

Hello! Meet the new me. I picked the name "Start Over Right" because it says exactly what I will do—take advantage of opportunities, choose positive friends, and think more in everything I do. Watch me. Remember I am new. I am Start Over Right!

The world is rich and I will earn my share. I will take enormous pleasure in making more money, accumulating more wealth, and associating with new friends who, too, want more of the good life. Most important of all, I will take immense satisfaction in winning the full respect of those who need me and follow my example.

To start my new life, I said good-bye to those who counseled me, "Be satisfied with what you have," "choose small goals because you can't reach large ones," "only cheaters get to the top," and "you're a good person but you haven't got what it takes."

In my new beginning, I have made a commitment to be captain of my economic fate. And this decision makes me feel very good about myself and those close to me.

## Guidelines for Thinking More in Key Situations

The more philosophy works. Its practice delivers results and provides great satisfaction. Tell yourself right now,

"I'm going to use it every day to go where I want, be the best I can, and enjoy being a winner.

Begin by dividing your life into its logical compartments. Then, as you shape your personal program for progress, refer often to the mental reinforcers given below:

## Focus on Creative Success at Work

1. Do what you really like to do. Life is too short to spend it in economic slavery.

2. Choose work where reward is based on performance. Don't be cheated. Don't subsidize lazy, indifferent people.

3. Select work that makes you truly captain of your economic fate.

4. Perform activities that build your pride and self-esteem. You must please yourself before you can please others.

## Focus on Building Friendships That Reward

1. Enjoy friends who are wise and see a Golden Age emerging. Avoid people who believe a new Dark Age lies ahead.

2. Avoid chronic pessimists. They have no place in your life.

3. Select friends who enrich you, elevate you, and give you real encouragement.

4. Pick friends who want to share profit-making ideas, success, and the fun of living.

## Focus on Psychological Environmental Control

1. Remember, your mind becomes what you feed it. Eat mental garbage and become a fool; feed your mind quality nourishment and it will work amazing miracles for you.

2. Concentrate on receiving and digesting good news. Don't pollute your mind with media-manufactured "crises."

3. Read, listen to, and watch information that makes you feel good toward yourself and other human beings.

4. Get your advice from successful people. Failures can only teach you how to fail.

## Focus on Getting Where You Want to Go

1. Set goals that really challenge you. Achieving the easy is no fun. Doing what others say is impossible is enormously satisfying.

2. Continually upgrade your goals. If your goals are the same today as a year ago, you are falling behind.

3. Remember, without goals you are a member of the living dead.

4. Keep in mind, goals are a source of energy, not a drain on your stamina. Setting big goals creates the energy to achieve them.

## Focus on Wealth Accumulation

1. Remember, the only wealth you have is money that is working to make more money.

2. Regardless of what you earn, at least 10 percent (ideally, 25 percent) should be put to work in your wealth-accumulation program.

3. Wealth accumulation is a great confidence builder. So build your wealth and you build your inner strength.

4. Be smart. Pay twice as much and buy half as many. Buy quality, not quantity.

YOU HAVE CROSSED THE
BAY. THE OCEAN LIES AHEAD.
SAIL IT TO THE LAND OF MORE!

# Index

# HYPNOSIS

## WHAT IT IS

## HOW TO USE IT

LEWIS R. WOLBERG, M.D.

# HYPNOSIS MAY BE JUST THE ANSWER YOU'VE BEEN SEARCHING FOR

*After years of research by some of the greatest minds in the world into the uses and benefits of hypnosis, its mighty influence has become legendary.*

*Hypnosis: What It Is and How to Use It* is a concise guide to the merits and limitations of modern hypnosis as an aid to health. It takes you behind the mysterious image of hypnosis, enabling you to make rational decisions about pursuing this form of therapy. Written in a clear and easily understood style, using case studies and Q & A's, it explores

- how hypnosis works
- various hypnotic methods
- the relationship between hypnotist and patient
- stage hypnosis
- use of hypnosis in medicine, surgery, dentistry, and mental health

and discusses how hypnosis can

- relieve and help you understand the reasons for a wide variety of emotional and physical conditions — from anxiety, depression, phobias, and compulsions to sleep disturbances, headaches, asthma, digestive problems
- relieve pain
- eliminate unwanted habits
- improve sexual performance and enjoyment
- enhance learning, memory, athletic performance

The book answers such interesting questions as: Who can be hypnotized and who can't? What does it feel like to be hypnotized? How can you tell when a person is hypnotized? It also contains a summary of the fascinating history of hypnosis, and a complete glossary of terms.

Cover Design by Peter Thorpe and Melvin Powers

**Louis R. Wolberg, M.D.** was a leading authority on hypnosis and pioneered its use for over 50 years. He was clinical professor of psychiatry at New York University School of Medicine, and the founder and dean emeritus of the Postgraduate Center for Mental Health.

WILSHIRE BOOK COMPANY
9731 Variel Avenue
Chatsworth, California 91311
320 Pages . . . $12.00

# THE LAW  OF  SUCCESS

## IN SIXTEEN LESSONS

# NAPOLEON HILL

*I invite you to meet an extraordinary princess and accompany her on an enlightening journey. You will laugh with her and cry with her, learn with her and grow with her . . . and she will become a dear friend you will never forget.*

*Marcia Grad Powers*

## 1 MILLION COPIES SOLD WORLDWIDE

# The Princess Who Believed in Fairy Tales

"Here is a very special book that will guide you lovingly into a new way of thinking about yourself and your life so that the future will be filled with hope and love and song."

**OG MANDINO**
**Author, *The Greatest Salesman in the World***

*The Princess Who Believed in Fairy Tales* by Marcia Grad is a personal growth book of the rarest kind. It's a delightful, humor-filled story you will experience so deeply that it can literally change your feelings about yourself, your relationships, and your life.

The princess's journey of self-discovery on the Path of Truth is an eye-opening, inspiring, empowering psychological and spiritual journey that symbolizes the one we all take through life as we separate illusion from reality, come to terms with our childhood dreams and pain, and discover who we really are and how life works.

If you have struggled with childhood pain, with feelings of not being good enough, with the loss of your dreams, or if you have been disappointed in your relationships, this book will prove to you that happy endings—and new beginnings—are always possible. Or, if you simply wish to get closer to your own truth, the princess will guide you.

The universal appeal of this book has resulted in its translation into numerous languages.

### Excerpts from Readers' Heartfelt Letters

"*The Princess* is truly a gem! Though I've read a zillion self-help and spiritual books, I got more out of this one than from any other one I've ever read. It is just too illuminating and full of wisdom to ever be able to thank you enough. The friends and family I've given copies to have raved about it."

"*The Princess* is powerful, insightful, and beautifully written. I am seventy years old and have seldom encountered greater wisdom. I've been waiting to read this book my entire life. You are a psychologist, a guru, a saint, and an angel all wrapped up into one. I thank you with all my heart."

Available wherever books are sold or send $12.00 (CA res. $12.99) plus $2.00 S/H to Wilshire Book Co., 9731 Variel Avenue, Chatsworth, California 91311-4315

For our complete catalog, visit our Web site at www.mpowers.com.

# Books by U.S. Andersen

## THE SECRET OF SECRETS

1. The Core of the Problem  2. The Secret of Secrets  3. The True Principle of Action  4. A Method for Mastery  5. Peace of Mind  6. Health and Well-Being  7. Loving and Being Loved  8. Success and Achievement  9. Creativeness  10. Staying Young Forever  11. Mystic Powers of the Mind  12. Mastery Over Life

320 Pages . . . $10.00

## THE MAGIC IN YOUR MIND

1. The Hidden Cause of All Things  2. Discovering the Secret Self  3. The Greatest Magic of All  4. Self-Mastery  5. Mind Over Matter  6. Mental Imagery  7. The Power of Choice  8. Overcoming Opposition  9. Developing Skills  10. Creating Your Own Talent  11. How to Use Your Sixth Sense  12. The Mental Attitude That Never Fails

256 Pages . . . $15.00

## SUCCESS-CYBERNETICS

1. Cybernetics: Science of Success. How to Use the new Science of Success Cybernetics. How to Find and Develop Your Greatest Potential. How to Set Your Self-Concept to Switch on Success.  2. The Cybernetics Success-Training Program How to Design Your Own Automatic Success Mechanism. How to Train the Success Mechanism into Your Nervous System. How to Constantly Improve Your Skills and Abilities.  3. The Cybernetics of Solving Problems. How to Rocket Your Brain Power up into Orbit. How to Use the Technique of Imagineering Ideas. How to Find Inside Solutions to Unsolvable Problems.  4. The Cybernetics of Handling People. How to Push-Button People into Fast Action. How to Persuade People to Your Point of View. How to Dynamite the Success Block Between People's Ears. How to Quick-shift Adversity into Achievement. How to Make Yourself into an Opportunity Magnet. How to Use a Great Secret That Brings Lasting Happiness.

272 Pages . . . $7.00

Available wherever books are sold or from the publisher.
Please add $2.00 shipping and handling for each book ordered.

### Wilshire Book Company
9731 Variel Avenue, Chatsworth, California 91311

For our complete catalog, visit our Web site at www.mpowers.com.

Treat Yourself to This Fun, Inspirational Book and Discover How to
Find Happiness and Serenity . . . No Matter What Life Dishes Out

# The Dragon Slayer
# With a Heavy Heart

*This new book by bestselling author Marcia Powers promises to be
one of the most important you will ever read—and one of the most
entertaining, uplifting, and memorable.*

*It brings the Serenity Prayer—which for years has been the guiding
light of 12-step programs worldwide—to everyone . . . and teaches
both new and longtime devotees how to apply it most effectively to
their lives.*

Sometimes things happen we wish hadn't. Sometimes things *don't*
happen we wish *would*. In the course of living, problems arise, both
big and small. We might wish our past had been different or that *we*
could be different. We struggle through disappointments and
frustrations, losses and other painful experiences.

As hard as we may try to be strong, to have a good attitude, not to
let things get us down, we don't always succeed. We get upset. We
worry. We feel stressed. We get depressed. We get angry. We do the
best we can and wait for things to *get* better so we can *feel* better. In
the meantime, our hearts may grow heavy . . . perhaps very heavy.

That's what happened to Duke the Dragon Slayer. In fact, *his*
heart grew *so* heavy with all that was wrong, with all that was not the
way it should be, with all that was unfair, that he became desperate to
lighten it—and set forth on the Path of Serenity to find out how.

Accompany Duke on this life-changing adventure. His guides will
be your guides. His answers will be your answers. His tools will be
your tools. His success will be your success. And by the time he is
heading home, both Duke and you will know how to take life's inevitable lumps and bumps in stride—and find happiness and serenity
anytime . . . even when you really, REALLY wish some things were
different.

"A BEAUTIFUL, EXCEPTIONALLY WELL-WRITTEN STORY THAT CAN HELP
EVERYONE TO BECOME EMOTIONALLY STRONGER AND BETTER ABLE TO
COPE WITH ADVERSITY."
Albert Ellis, Ph.D.
President, Albert Ellis Institute
Author of *A Guide to Rational Living*

Available wherever books are sold or send $12.00 (CA res. $12.99) plus $2.00 S/H
to Wilshire Book Co., 9731 Variel Avenue, Chatsworth, CA 91311-4315.

For our complete catalog, visit our Web site at www.mpowers.com.

*For every man who wants to shed his armor—and for the women who care about them...*

# KNIGHTS WITHOUT ARMOR

If you are struggling to rid yourself of heavy old restrictive armor that limits pleasure and joy in your life, hurts your relationships, damages your health, causes you to do destructive things to yourself and others—or if someone you care about is engaged in this struggle—*Knights Without Armor* is for you.

For centuries men have been taught from childhood that encasing themselves in armor is an integral part of being a man. And some men are further trapped by roles and jobs that demand they be tough and cold and hard as steel. They use psychological armor to forge ahead and to protect themselves from the potential ravages of what they confront day after day.

For many, maintaining their armor results in their walling themselves off from their feelings and from other people, which can come at a very high cost—isolation, confusion, frustration, anger, depression, addictions, troubled relationships, stress-related illnesses. But they fear that if they remove their armor, they may lose their strength, their power—even their masculinity.

Not so! says *Knights Without Armor*. Living the myth of the lone hero who conquers all through the force of his will is not the *only* way—or the *best* way—to be strong and powerful. This book is an adventure of self-discovery for male readers. The "Twelve Tasks of Men" guides them past the problems they have opening up their lives, and the "Male Manifesto" clarifies what it means to be a man. The adventure for women is in gaining insight into their man's quest to find a new way to live in the world.

For a beautiful, 294-page hardcover edition of *Knights Without Armor: A Practical Guide for Men in Quest of the Masculine Soul* by Aaron R. Kipnis, Ph.D.—psychotherapist, leader of men's groups, and expert in modern man's quest to live a new masculine role—order online at www.mpowers.com or send $10.00 (CA res. $10.83) plus $2.00 S/H to Wilshire Book Company, 9731 Variel Avenue, Chatsworth, CA 91311-4315.

# How You Can Have Confidence and Power in Dealing with People

A major key to success in your business and personal life is knowing how to deal with people. In fact, studies have shown that knowing how to deal with people is 85 to 90 percent of business and professional success, and 90 to 95 percent of personal happiness.

Now here's some great news. Dealing effectively with people is a skill you can learn, just as you learned to ride a bicycle, drive an automobile, or play the piano.

Discover how you can get what you want and be the way you want to be by tapping into your hidden assets. Assets you may not even realize you have. Assets that can transform an ordinary person into an extraordinary one. Assets that can give you more confidence and personal power than you ever thought possible.

Find out how to

- Feel confident in any business or social situation
- Win others to your way of thinking
- Understand and get along with people
- Make it easy for people to like you
- Create a positive and lasting impression
- Help others feel comfortable and friendly — instantly
- Make new friends and keep them
- Find love and build relationships that work

The way you lived yesterday determined your today. But the way you live today will determine your tomorrow. Every day is a new opportunity to become the way you want to be and to have your life become what you want it to be.

Take the first step toward becoming all you're capable of being. Read Marcia Grad's book *Charisma*, which teaches a proven step-by-step plan to help anyone develop the ultimate in personal power. Then get ready for an incredible adventure that will change you and your life forever.